MANIFESTATIONS OF THOUGHT: WHEN THE DRAGON COMES

THE SELECTED WRITINGS OF SHAKA A. SHAKUR

1824
books

Published in November 2025 by
1804 Books, New York, NY

1804Books.com

This selection © 1804 Books, New York, NY
ISBN: 979-8-9990195-3-0
Library of Congress Control Number: 2025948493

Edited by Derek R. Ford and Tessa Kochert
Cover by Vivek Venkatraman

"Shakur reminds us that the prison is a site of war and his New Afrikan Independence Movement calls for those of us not behind the "iron curtain of the prison walls" to recognize that there is no meaningful clarification of Black life and existence without the involvement of those held within . . . Shakur is not teaching us what to think but how to think and to arrive at difficult and necessary conclusions. And as we are told, that we can read this book at all is a triumph, as it stands as testimony that Shakur is still here, still struggling, and we need to join him."

— *Jared Ball*
host of iMiXWHATiLiKE! *podcast,*
author of The Myth and Propaganda of Black Buying Power

"*Manifestations of Thought: When the Dragon Comes* is a searing collection of prison writings by New Afrikan revolutionary Shaka A. Shakur, composed from within the belly of the beast, America's carceral empire. A radical dialectic comes from solitary cells and surveillance-soaked prison blocks: fierce, grounded, and unflinchingly honest. These essays span personal transformation, revolutionary theory, critiques of patriarchy, and the urgent call for freedom, dignity and liberation. Edited with care, this volume is a political arsenal and a moral compass for resistance."

— *Suchitra Vijayan*
author of How Long Can the Moon Be Caged:
Voices of Indian Political Prisoners

"This book proves what comrades of the struggle already knew: Shaka Shakur is a guerilla intellectual of the highest order. Carrying on the political tradition of New Afrikan/Black liberation through sober analysis, precise criticism, and theoretical clarity, the thoughts of the dragon manifest as armed and dangerous in this revolutionary call to action."

— *D. Musa Springer*
Walter Rodney Foundation, host of the Groundings *podcast*

"What an impressive highly insightful and moving book. Brother Shaka gives a broad picture of his life journey while also being unjustly incarcerated. A must read."

— *Emory Douglas*
Social Justice Artist

TABLE OF CONTENTS

This book is dedicated to my moms, Leola Jones; my son Jela Simba Shakur a.k.a Mark Lasenby; and my wife Akili Shakur, who has been my ride or die for over twenty years.

EDITORIAL INTRODUCTION

The fact this book has made it to publication—that you're holding these words on paper, seeing them on a screen, or hearing them out loud—is evidence that the state's escalating efforts to silence Shaka Adiyia Shakur, to isolate him, prevent him from organizing, stop his role in developing a new generation of fighters for justice, have failed. As Shaka details in the following pages, the politically motivated efforts range from the publicly overt to the discreetly subtle. He's been kidnapped, without due process or any warning, and forced into domestic exile hundreds of miles away from his family and community, forced to spend over a decade in solitary confinement, beaten by guards and lackeys, and more. Yet in some ways it's the less overt, seemingly mundane attacks he's forced to navigate daily and hourly, that are in some ways the most troubling.

It was one year ago when comrades and I lost touch with Shaka. For almost a year, we were communicating by phone and email at least once a day. Then, radio silence. Finally, we learned he was ambushed by prison authorities, ripped from his cell at Beaumont Correctional Facility, and transferred to another nearby prison. We didn't hear from Shaka because they put him in solitary confinement, trapping him in a cell for nine days. He had no running water; the only water he could access came from the rain that flooded his cell. When we finally spoke, he asked me to tell comrades that the entire time he never doubted they were struggling for his freedom and all of Our people's freedom. Unable to even speak to his wife for over a week, his knowledge of the self-mobilization of those on the outside provided some comfort.

The prisoncrats at Beaumont were setting Shaka up for some time. They would get inmates to hassle him. If he was on a video call, it wouldn't be long before people started walking closely by the monitor, leaning slightly over his shoulder to peer into the screen. The guards routinely left his cell unlocked at night, and it wasn't long before a small "gang" of young inmates robbed Shaka and his cellie. Shaka didn't take the bait and he didn't snitch. He did what he could to work it out amongst his fellow inmates. But eventually Shaka was physically provoked and fought back, providing the justification for another short stint in solitary confinement and an abrupt move to Buckingham Correctional Facility.

By the time Black August started in 2024, Shaka still hadn't received his legal and other personal materials from the warden of Beaumont, Mariea LeFevers. Notably, LeFevers was the warden of the Fluvanna Correctional Center for Women until April 2023, when she was suddenly replaced after a string of inmate deaths at the prison came to light, followed by several civil suits against LeFevers.[1]

LeFevers and her staff at Beaumont continued withholding key legal materials from Shaka, including two DVDs and seven thumb drives—not to mention his books, writings, and other property. It took a concerted effort to force her to turn these items over.

This last year at Buckingham, Shaka has been subjected to the intentional circulation of false narratives and verbal insults by correctional officers and their lackey inmates. Those visiting Shaka aren't immune either. Staff have reported car keys that were "mysteriously" missing after a visit. Most egregiously, when his wife, Akili Shakur, traveled from Gary, Indiana, to visit him for the weekend, she was only allowed a single ninety-minute visit with her loving husband. Yet anyone who communicates with Shaka is targeted. His tablet and email accounts are routinely hacked, emails disappeared, passwords changed, and the list goes on.

As such, this book's publication is a victory in many ways, a win by Shaka and his supporters, mentors, family, New Afrikan and multinational comrades, and the organizations he's built and supported. First, insofar as his most important pieces, written from numerous prisons and formerly scattered across various platforms, are now cohesively assembled and revised in one place. For the working and oppressed of the world, the most important victory is that the following ideas and proposals, which are based on historical study and ongoing, collective practice and reflection, are widely accessible to all those fighting for socialism and the national liberation of New Afrika and all oppressed peoples in the u.s. and across the world.

Manifestations of Thought contains a series of some of Shaka's most significant personal, theoretical, organizational, and practical writings. Working together—as Shaka always does—We collectively selected, organized, and edited each essay in this book, giving serious consideration to what to include and omit. The organization and rhythm of the book are also the products of a collective orchestra. The harmonics of the book are composed of pieces written since the turn of the century, but its beat goes further back.

As Shaka details in the opening chapter, his politicization happened in the 1980s. By the next decade, Shaka was notorious throughout Indiana prisons for his organizational capabilities. In 1996, Shaka was one of the "Indiana Six" who faced serious charges for organizing inside and outside, across national lines, against the impending execution of Ziyon Ishva Yisrayah ("Tommie Smith").[2] The day before he and other New Afrikan Political Prisoners were snatched and rounded up SWAT-style by heavily-armed prison guards, Shaka had organized an action in which "approximately 150 prisoners of all nationalities ate their afternoon meal in complete silence to protest the premeditated murder of an innocent man."[3] This is just one example among many, and in each instance the idea of gaining his individual "freedom" from prison at the expense of his comrades in the struggle for all of Our freedom would never enter his mind.

Terminology and Editorial Notes

Due to the continuous and dynamic ways that the state tries to limit Shaka's ability to communicate with those of us on the outside, Shaka's initial writings are often comprised of various abbreviations and forms of shorthand which we have translated into their longer form. More importantly, because this book is intended to speak beyond the existing ranks of the New Afrikan struggle, we sought to strike a balance between adhering to the intentional spelling and capitalization of words and phrases in that evolving tradition and the reader who may be entirely new but open to the National Liberation project.

The terminology of the New Afrikan Independence Movement is a political matter. As Sanyika Shakur notes, the politics arises from the needed "to distinguish, apply energy, weight, and clarity to the ongoing and ever-increasing need for sharper, more critical words to describe the socioeconomic phenomena of national oppression."[4] Precisely because this book seeks to advance *and* expand that struggle, we have maintained some traditional spellings and other phrasings. All readers can consult the political glossary (adapted from the Black Liberation Army's "Political Dictionary") in the book for definitions of certain terms. For readers newer to the New Afrikan Independence Movement, we want to mention a few upfront.

First, the u.s., amerika, british, and other words are not capitalized because they are not proper nouns; they do not denote legal entities like nations. They are, in fact, illegal. Second, not only amerika but Afrika and other words traditionally spelled with a "c" are instead spelled with a "k." Afrikan linguistics rendered the sound with a "k" until european colonialists changed it to a "c." spelled with a "K" instead of a "C" to root our National Identity in Afrika, whose linguists first used "K" to indicate the "C" sound in English. Third, words that refer to collectives are capitalized while those referring to the individual are decapitalized. This is because "We" are more important than "i" am, despite what the capitalist ideology of individualism tries to pump into our heads.

Most footnotes throughout the text were introduced by the editors to (1) identify the original date and outlet of publication; (2) provide background and other contextual information for newer readers; (3) explain the reasons behind some of the chapters; and, because Shaka doesn't always have access to his books, (4) provide accurate citations so the reader can easily follow lines of inquiry if they wish to do so. Each footnote not added by the editors is explicitly attributed to Shaka A. Shakur.

Along with Shaka and the Shaka Shakur Freedom Campaign, we want to thank 1804 Books and their editorial team for facilitating the timely publication of this work.

We want to thank the Shaka Shakur Freedom Foundation and the organizations and many people who supported and continue to support him as a father, grandfather, human, New Afrikan, Political Prisoner, human, and revolutionary theorist and organizer. Without you, we would be deprived of Shaka's invaluable mentorship, from which we have learned so much. Thank you, comrades.

Free Shaka A. Shakur and all Political Prisoners and Prisoners of War Now!

— *Derek R. Ford*

PREFACE

My comrade-brother in the struggle, Shaka A. Shakur, a New Afrikan Political Prisoner, freedom fighter, and theoretician of the New Afrikan Independence Movement (NAIM), releases a collection of essays and writings at a critical time of political, social, dialectical, and ideological development and struggle for future activist and revolutionaries.

Manifestations of Thought. The title speaks for itself. This book, divided into four different sections, takes you on the journey of his own constant development and, at the same time, on this journey within Our own personal development. As a result, We can use it to sharpen Our political and social consciousness, to develop ideas that We can apply to the worldly material paradoxes that lead to the road of National Liberation for New Afrikan People and other neocolonized people striving to break the chains of neo-imperialism.

You ever heard the saying, "Iron sharpens iron?" Well, this is the political toolbox to sharpen your spear—or thoughts—consciously.

Shaka is the New Afrikan Scientist that continues to remind Us that Our greatest minds, though captured behind the gulag walls, continue the legacy and struggle of the Dragon George Jackson and other New Afrikan/Black freedom fighters who have built universities on the basis of study and struggle despite the brutal repression from Our historical enemies in prisons across the amerika.

The reader will experience through Shaka's writings how the Prison Industrial Complex (PIC) and neocolonial system of amerika works hand-in-hand with an ecosystem of war and assault on Our minds and existence outside the walls and inside the walls. Fascist slavery is not just imposed on those who are physically in prisons. Amerika is prison.

This book also reminds Us why We must get back to building study units and develop cadres, which are the foundation of NAIM. Developing theory is essential to practice, and Shaka shows Us how and demonstrates with his words, thoughts, and intellect—some of his own weapons that he utilizes to uplift and guide a new generation of activists and revolutionaries to prepare them for Our historical duty.

Manifestations of Thought would be summed up in one description:

> Your spear is your intellect, your wit, your stamina, your ability to advance. Your shield is your strength to ward off, evade, defend & shelter yourself. In tandem they are your weapons of struggle.
>
> In every metaphor of life's struggle, whether against the elements of nature, or oppression from humans on humans, the spear and the shield can be used. Your tactical knowledge at any given time will instruct you whether to thrust your spear or raise your shield.
>
> Whether to go on the offensive or to retreat. In order to have this consciousness you'll need to be in tune with objective reality.[5]

These are words from Our Comrade-Brother Sanyika Shakur that I echo into the soul of the reader!

Don't just read this book. Use it and study it to develop a political, revolutionary, social consciousness as you join the struggle. Comrade George Jackson lives and the Dragon never dies.[6] Shaka is breathing historical fire of thoughts in the whirlwind to preserve revolutionary Dragons' blood while his spear is in the throat of amerikan fascism.

— *Haki Kweli Shakur*
August Third Collective NAIM
Stand Up Struggle Forward!
59 ADM

INTRODUCTION

This book, *Manifestations of Thought*, represents another stage and qualitative leap in my continued development. This collection of writings and essays is an attempt to not only continue to add my voice to the continued political discussions and dialogue taking place in various quarters, but also to continue adding my voice to the theoretical development of future revolutionary cadre and up-and-coming generations of future activists who made (or will make) a conscious decision to challenge this corrupt capitalist-imperialist beast that We call a government.

This is also an attempt to reinforce the statement that Comrade George Jackson's cellmate stated over fifty years ago that "every goodbye ain't gone." That even from behind enemy lines, even from behind the iron curtain of the amerikan gulag/Prison Industrial Complex, We can still make a contribution towards the forward motion of this struggle.[7] That although We are locked down and caged, We have a role in this Struggle, in this war.

It has been fifty-plus years since the murder and assassination of Comrade George, and yet We speak of him and his words as if he is still physically here. The state still deems him a threat and enemy of the state while prison administrations across the country continue to ban his books and writings.

Section I, "The Personal is Political," is an attempt to communicate that everything is political or dialectical. You often hear people say, "I'm not into politics." When in actuality, there's no way around it, because We are social beings. We live in and under a system and in a material world where every choice and decision is a political decision, choice, and a reflection of social consciousness or the lack thereof, even when We think it is a choice of free will.

Where do ideas come from, how does consciousness form? Our interactions with the material world help to shape and mold that developing consciousness and the decisions and choices that We make. That within itself represents a manifestation of a political expression.

Section II is named "History, Theory, Practice" because it is important for me to try and explain the historical development of the New Afrikan Nation and why and how Black/New Afrikan folks in the u.s. constitute a Nation.

It explains how and why We as a people and a neocolonized people have a right both to Self-Determination and National Independence. It is also important to establish the Historical Continuity of Our Struggle as a people from the shores of the Motherland to the shores of Babylon and the Western Hemisphere.

It just as important to understand that, in order to fight for a better day, a better world, you must have a vision and you must have an overstanding of historical materialism and a vision not only of what you're fighting for, but an overstanding of history, of Our story, so that We don't repeat the same ole mistakes or repeat *his* story. We are not fighting to be free only to install a continuation of neocolonialism under a flag of independence.

Although i do not believe that the United Nations represents a legitimate democratic institution that genuinely represent all nations equally—or even genuinely represent the interests of the colonial and neocolonized nations of oppressive imperialist powers—its own laws and resolutions that establish international law recognize that New Afrikan people represent a Nation without a state and have the right to Independence, Autonomy, and Self-Determination.

International law as defined by the UN states that a colonial power doesn't have the right to impose second class citizenship upon a formerly colonized or conquered people. That is what the u.s. did with its emancipation proclamation and constitutional amendments.

Another reason for the title of Section II is because social, political, military theory, and science are what guide Our practice. How do We determine if a theory is correct in its analysis, assessment, and application? How do We determine if it's true and correct? We determine it by applying it to concrete conditions, i.e., by putting theory into practice and separating theory from mere rhetoric. This is why We don't just engage in theory alone: Armchair revolutionaries with all of the answers, but ain't in the trenches, ain't in the mud, ain't on the block or in the hood. How can We advance the Struggle forward if We don't have boots on the ground? If We don't have programs, institutions, infrastructure, resources, strategies, and tactics? Debate, Ideological Struggle are all necessary to advance Us forward, none of which are possible without practice.

The New Afrikan Nation and NAIM are like a spicy gumbo. Some people can't eat spicy food, so you got to feed 'em something else that is just as tasty to satisfy those hunger pains, and that is what Our Struggle is about on some levels. We are not only trying to increase the appetite of Our people: We are trying to satisfy the thirst and hunger pains of Our people for freedom and liberation.

In order to prevail We must have correct theoretical development and practice.

Section III is called the "Prison Industrial Complex" because a lot of folks don't see the intersectionality and connection with/between the Prison Industrial Complex (PIC), the Military Industrial Complex, globalization, and genocide. Outside of intellectualism, a lot of people really don't see the PIC as the continuation of modern-day slavery and genocide because more and more "people of color" are forced not only to work within them, but are confined within their cages. Our labor on both sides is exploited in the interests of parasitic capitalism and imperialism. These colonized folks that are forced to work in and help maintain their (prisons) existence and function; whose labor is exploited just as well as part of the working class that has its parasitic component in maintaining that neocolonization.

The struggle around the PIC and prison abolitionism are equally as important as the larger struggle. These are Our institutions of higher learning, base camps of the future, and unfortunately it is also where all too many of you are coming!

Those of Us trapped behind enemy lines have to be supported and liberated, and people have to become more serious and strategic in how this monster is viewed—especially those of you with educational and skin privileges! It's called a "complex" for a reason!

Section IV is called "Continuing the Struggle." This section is Our attempt to connect the dots and *explain* the intersections of imperialist oppression with or through an internationalist lens. It is also an attempt to communicate that a more direct and serious approach must be undertaken when confronting these current realities.

I mean, the magnitude of people being slaughtered in the interest of global imperialist domination and profit is sickening. The war kkkrimes being committed on a scale not seen since World War II and these rogue states and multinational corporations that function like nation-states are allowed to function as business as usual, and with diplomatic immunity from international tribunals, international law, or sanctions from such recognized bodies.

There has to be a more effective way to address these situations and bring to heel such rogue and oppressive governments!

Conclusion

Let this introduction and the herein included writings be more ideological and theoretical fuel to the necessary ongoing discussions and ideological struggle around critical issues such as revolutionary nationalism, national liberation struggles, the right to self-determination, and the reality of patriarchy. Let the following ignite struggles around the class contradictions both within the New Afrikan Nation and outside of it as We relate to and interact with the settler-colonial imperialist state known as amerika.

These are both serious and critical times for poor, struggling, working-class people in general and those of oppressed nations in particular.

Hopefully, one of the things that these writings can accomplish is to further shine the spotlight on revolutionary activist Political Prisoners (PPs), help people to overstand the critical and decisive role of prisoners within the larger struggle, and relay the critical need for building genuine and principled inside/outside and mutual-aid type of relationships.

We as prisoners and PPs in particular don't want to be "saved" or "rescued" within the paternalistic politic of missionaries. We don't want to be placed on no pedestal or given no celebrity status behind the walls.

We want acknowledgement and respect for Our ideas and contributions. We want to focus on the roles of strategies, tactics, and on how to get the work done—from reentry to mental health treatment and beyond.

References to PPs and the PIC are not meant for intellectual masturbation or the obligatory shout out. No, We need an on-the-ground movement that has boots in Our streets and is not dependent on the good will of some politician trying to get reelected. The same energy We see around the struggle to Free Palestine We need around mass incarceration, parole, liberation of Our elders, the overturning "three-strikes laws," etc.

Free Palestine!! But also Free Haiti!! Free the Congo and the Sudan!! Nations and communities that nobody wants to talk about, even a lot of Our "allies" on the left. Why is that? i'm sorry, i digress.

But why are only safe forms of struggle considered when focusing on these prisons and the PIC while companies like the GEO Group gross $1 billion a year in profits? A company that has no fear of a divestment campaign against it similar to the anti-Apartheid movement that targeted companies that invested in and propped up the racist regime in South Afrika?

Let these writings contribute to the broader discussions of prisons and the right to Self-Determination and Independence. Let them be ammunition for deeper discussions around prison abolitionism, dual power projects, policing and self-empowerment, alternatives to imprisonment, and dismantling the beast as We know it, as We struggle and strive to breakdown petty superficial differences amongst Ourselves. Ideological and Class Struggle are Necessary!!

— Shaka A. Shakur

SECTION I:
THE PERSONAL IS POLITICAL

CHAPTER 1

MANY ARE CALLED BUT FEW ARE CHOSEN

My name is Shaka Adiyia Shakur, and i am a conscious, woke New Afrikan Political Prisoner (PP) and Prison Activist. i am fifty-eight years old and embarking upon my twenty-third year in captivity on trumped-up and politically motivated charges for a wrongful conviction: the attempted murder of a Gary, Indiana cop.[8]

When i was first asked to write a short biography about my struggles and legal battles in an attempt to raise funds and critical support for myself and another comrade, i was stuck. i couldn't wrap my head around it. . . . there really is no short version of this saga.

So, i'm going to put this in the context of mental health, which is an area that doesn't get enough attention for both former prisoners and PPs released after being tortured and dehumanized. The issues of Post-Traumatic Stress Disorder (PTSD) and the lack of real reentry preparation are rarely talked about.

In August of 2001, after having just served a total of seventeen years in prison—including in the notorious Super-Maximum Security Prison in Boscobel, Wisconsin, it was the day after my birthday. My teenage son and only child was murdered barely thirty minutes after having called me to come pick him up. It was the first sole day in eighteen years that i would have spent on the streets with him. Seeing his body splattered across the hot summer asphalt from two shotgun blasts to the back, triggered an avalanche of emotions and events for me. How do i explain to my two-month-old granddaughter that her father had just been murdered?

At the time of his murder, i had only been home for ten months. i was attending Purdue University full-time while working in the Upward Bound TRIO program at Purdue University Northwest. i was also giving lectures and workshop tours at various colleges and schools on topics like Supermax Torture and Human Rights Violations in u.s. Prisons. i spoke at Princeton University, Temple University, the University of Wisconsin-Madison, and many others. i was also active in community organizing efforts.

After my son's murder and flushing his killer(s) to the surface, i started to self-medicate. My mental health deteriorated.

I was initially imprisoned at the age of sixteen and served four tours in various Indiana Supermax and Control Unit Prisons. All of those years being chained to beds and poles in stress positions, being left in trip gear chained to other prisoners, being subjected to the fire hosings, the tear gassings, the wars; it all kicked in. i became reckless and self-destructive, no longer caring whether i lived or died. The PTSD symptoms i was experiencing began to intensify and i fell into a deep depression.

Because of my investigation into my own son's murder and my and my partner's history of challenging and exposing the Gary Police Department for targeting and brutalizing Black Youth, i was consistently targeted by them. i was constantly pulled over, searched, checked for warrants, etc. Approximately five months after my son Jela's murder, i was accused of attempted murder of a Gary cop during a bogus traffic stop. A police cruiser took incoming rounds as the cop stood beside the open door; this cop dove into the car—actively being fired upon—and would later claim that I, or someone else, had tried to murder him. The forensic and physical evidence did not support the narrative or allegation of my attempted murder, and yet i was still wrongfully convicted and given a sixty-three-year sentence—because of the now-repealed three-strikes or enhanced sentencing guidelines. If they applied the laws to me today, i would have been released in at least 2021.

Contradictions

Returning to prison, specifically to the Indiana Reformatory where i had a long history of organizing resistance against the racist prison guard network and administration, i would be falsely accused of attempted murder of the director of Internal Affairs, Mike Rains.

After several months of campaigning against harassment during contact visits with my granddaughter, i subverted several security checkpoints and gates, and slipped into Rains' office to confront him. How could he deny reentry of my granddaughter after she had been consistently visiting for two years without any issues? An argument ensued, and i began destroying all of the computers in his office. i was armed as a countermeasure to the possibility of being beaten by responding officers.

I was charged with attempted murder, possession of a deadly weapon (knife), and ultimately forced to sign an illegal plea agreement for twenty years with eight years suspended—meaning i was sentenced to six of twelve years.

Rains conducted his own investigation into the alleged assault against him. He, as the alleged victim and Internal Affairs investigator, conducted the investigation, filed his own internal prison charges, and signed the conduct report. Based on his own investigation, he referred outside charges to be filed to the State Police investigator. This is a blatant conflict of interest!

In this small county, Rains was a local celebrity, having worked in the Department of Corrections (DOC) for over twenty years and filed outside charges against hundreds of prisoners, feeding the PIC with assembly-line, railroad "justice."

Fast forward approximately three to five years, and a huge scandal would break the news. A colleague and fellow investigator of Rains was busted for trafficking drugs and cell phones. This colleague flipped on Rains, exposing that for years Rains had been running a smuggling ring of drugs, phones, and more. So many guards were removed from the prison that there was no longer a system to operate, and since so many of the general staff members were lost, the prison as a whole couldn't be run . . . not Rains though!!

Rains was the John Edgar Hoover of the prison system. He had files on everyone, he knew where the bodies were buried, and therefore was never fired or sent to jail. Instead, he was demoted from a director position to a regular Internal Affairs position. He then moved next door to another prison, where he could quietly retire with a full pension!!

The DOC would demand that the probation portion of my sentence begin immediately. As part of this demand, if i caught certain types of prison tickets—having weapons or engaging in violence—the DOC could petition to have my probation violated and a twenty-year sentence imposed. However, the twelve-year sentence tied to my plea doesn't begin until i finish my original sixty-three-year sentence!! That is an illegal sentence. You can't run half of a sentence now and half of it later. The sentence must either be consecutive or concurrent. Since both the state and DOC demanded that the sentence begin immediately, the time portion should have also begun, and the sentence as a whole should have been completed.

In 2006, after returning to the Lake County Jail on a post-conviction release, i was exposed to and confronted by a rogue group of primarily white sheriff deputies and correctional officers (COs) who were targeting and beating the shit out of young Black men. This was common knowledge under, and on the watch of, the jail's first Black female warden.

As a jailhouse lawyer running a law clinic, helping young brothers with their cases and preventing them from signing their lives away on bogus pleas, and as an alleged attempted cop killer . . . i was targeted for a beating. On camera, i was attacked and defended myself against a squad of six guards. Off camera, i was handcuffed behind my back and carried into a segregation cell where i was beaten and stomped on. i required transportation to an outside hospital for imaging to determine if i had a broken jaw or eye socket fracture. Fortunately, i did not.

I would be given several bogus counts and other charges despite the fact that the attack was on video!

The state filed a habitual offender/three-strikes count, which could have further enhanced my sentence by thirty years if i was found guilty. i was given a sellout public defender who refused to even try to obtain the video tape! Left with no other choice, i took a plea on a battery case for two years and cut my losses.

We organized and protested in front of the jail and courthouse, calling for an investigation into these rogue elements. Nothing was done. The Department of Justice's Civil Rights Division requested copies of the tapes, but as a supposed "cop killer," they and the local authorities refused to act.

Fast forward several years later, and this same group of guards and others brutally beat a Black prisoner to the point of cardiac arrest. He had to be revived on the operating table. And the damn burst. This case was settled for over $1 million and opened a floodgate of lawsuits and investigations. The feds came in and uncovered both these assaults and more. At least eight guards were given felony charges, five of those eight would be the same ones who attacked me; they were all fired.

My case should be reopened and thrown out. From the beginning, i argued that i was attacked and defending myself, that this was a pattern of misconduct. The only reason i took a plea was that i did not trust the public defender to properly represent me. This statement is on record and part of the transcript.

With the current climate in the country and the demand for so-called criminal justice reform, me and comrades are working to expose and organize around Our convictions. We aim to spark interest among lawyers, activists, and the public to investigate Our cases. In my case, this is the new convictions received since being imprisoned for my original wrongful conviction.

It is these types of wrongful convictions and cases that need resources and assistance to expose and overturn. For everything i've written, i either have the documentation to substantiate it or is a matter of public record.

We appreciate your support and solidarity.

Dare to Struggle, Dare to Win!

CHAPTER 2

THE PERSONAL IS POLITICAL AND THE POLITICAL IS PERSONAL

The average person tends to see the political as something that is separate from self, as this whole little thing that can be placed into a box and turned on and off when u choose. No, everything is political. From the toilet paper We choose to wipe Our behinds with, to the toothpaste We choose to brush Our teeth with—it is all a political act and statement. The very choice to even use toilet paper as We know it is a political act and not just a personal choice. (We are subjects of marketing, advertising, etc.)

Lay people and non-conscious people tend to see and read politics as what We see politicians and the system practicing. We are social beings and We live and exist in a social world where some form or degree of social interaction is necessary. This social dialectic, this social interaction, is colored by Our politics, which is manifested through the personal. As social beings. We have also been socialized based on Our interaction with the material world, as social beings, Our socialization is what gives rise and shapes us as such. As children, as boys and girls, we are immediately socialized into gender roles of male and female and what girls and boys can and can't do or should and shouldn't do. This holds for what is or isn't acceptable to society, whether it be sports, the workplace, or personal relationships. This reflects a politic, which gives rise to a culture and cultural expressions. i don't want to get all technical and philosophical. i just want to point out what should be obvious on some levels, especially for those of Us that embrace a radical politic.

There's a quote that, to paraphrase, goes: "once you become conscious there is no such thing as unconscious, from there on, there is only betrayal."

What We bring to personal relationships—the way We love and a host of other practices—may be in a personal context, but they still reflect a certain politic, political development, or lack thereof. This leads me to trying to overstand some people's recent criticisms of a protest We had outside of the warden's house for the Westville Correctional Facility where, at last report, six prisoners have died as a result of being infected with COVID-19 and this warden's negligent and oppressive policies; where, at last report, the prison had a 0.92 percent infection rate with over fifty guards infected. This is a situation so dire that the state moved in the National Guard to perform critical services and beef up security. This is while the warden is being vicious and oppressive, being indifferent to the conditions that the prisoners are being held in. The buck stops with him!

So, Our Prison Solidarity Coalition spearheaded by the New Afrikan Black Panther Party (NABPP) held a protest in front of his house with body bags and bullhorns while live streaming it. Some people said this was too personal and We should not pull his neighbors into it. i really find this position extremely disgusting, seriously. Like i-want-to-vomit disgusting.

How are the crimes this man is committing, the international laws of human rights that he is violating . . . not personal? Are you really trying to suggest that he is just doing his job? That after office hours he should be able to return back home to the safety and sanctity of his house and neighborhood in peace?

"Hi honey, I'm home, how was your day?"

"Ah, I just weaponized COVID-19 and cross-contaminated hundreds of prisoners. I had to have some of them beaten for trying to go against me. You know just another day on the job!"

With this rationale, why do We protest killer cops? Why do We protest u.s. soldiers who torture and kill civilians?

The Struggle is Personal and Political

People in positions of power or authority, people who are supposed to have the people's trust and who they are supposed to represent should not be allowed to commit crimes against humanity. They should not be able to hide behind a badge, behind the color of law and commit murder or other atrocities. They should not be allowed to hide in plain sight. So, yea, We should throw body bags on their lawns and educate their neighbors as to what exists amongst them.

You know, reactionaries come out against sex offenders or ex-cons living in their communities, but not people who commit torture, not war criminals or racists who allow death to happen in their name, who allow beatings and infectious diseases to spread like wildfire in their prisons on their watch.

So, for the critics and from someone that has been down for twenty years and putting in work for over thirty: You damn right its personal!

Today it's body bags on the lawns. Who is to say what it might be tomorrow?! And that, my friend, is the political statement that We are trying to make!!

If mass murderers and tyrants that were or are in positions of power weren't allowed to live in plain sight without being challenged, We might live in a better world and society today.

People need to pick a side or get out of the way. You cannot turn your politics on and off like a light switch, and you can't keep trying to play by the state/system rules that you claim to be committed to removing.

You say it's too personal. Tell that to the families of brothers and sisters who are being suffocated by killer cops on amerika's streets. Tell that to the families of prisoners who are dying lonely deaths in cages and infirmary beds from COVID-19. The position is just wrong on so many levels.

Pick a side. It's gonna get real!!

CHAPTER 3

THE PEN IS A WEAPON

For one who is oppressed and has a conscious mind, the act of writing is a subversive act. This is especially true for someone in prison, trapped behind enemy lines.

The art and desire to write, like the desire to scream, must come from a space: a space of liberation—a liberatory act of resistance.

For me, writing has always been therapeutic—a salve against the blows and wounds inflicted by abusive power. It has also been a tool, a weapon, if you will, to bludgeon and beat back the beast that strives to steal my mind, crush my soul, and destroy my spirit and will to live and fight.

When i was young, my approach to fighting my battles was always physical. i never realized that little letters, matched together to form words and sentences, could have the power of an atom bomb, the power to shape minds, move mountains, and topple oppressive regimes.

Who knew that men and womyn with fancy titles, in skirts and ties, with an array of weapons and devices at their fingertips, would plot, plan, and scheme on how to silence such words, to erase, delete, and prohibit the writing or speaking of such words. Tyranny knows no bounds.

Why do such elite people fear an old man trapped in a concrete box behind a solid steel door? Because those little, tiny letters, those characters that form words, sentences, and paragraphs, give birth to *knowledge*.

Knowledge in the hands of the oppressed, the dispossessed, the disinherited, and the disenchanted is like kryptonite to those who wield oppressive power.

CHAPTER 4

THE COLDNESS OF THE SYSTEM AND THE WARMTH OF RESISTANCE

They say there can be no greater appreciation of the light unless you have been through the deepest darkness. Becoming conscious—politically and socially aware—has become the greatest light for me. There is no greater brilliance or radiance than awakening from the mental slumber that is the lack of knowledge.

There is power in the genius, commitment, and mobilization of the people. It is not, as capitalism would have Us believe, about vulgar materialism, the collection of things, and the sexual conquest or control and domination over other peoples.

How is it that We live in a society where everyone is supposed to be free, yet so many are alienated from their sense of self, self-medicating in some form, or seeking to escape the social reality in which they exist? How is it that We supposedly live in such a great democracy, with so much parasitic privilege, yet We have millions that are working, poor, homeless, or in cages? There must be a contradiction in the lies and propaganda We are being spoon-fed.

The ability to be a critical thinker and to perform a critical analysis represents one of the greatest strengths We have as human beings—and one of the greatest threats to oppressive power.

These are the early morning musings of a PP embarking upon his nineteenth year trapped behind enemy lines.

CHAPTER 5

MOVING TOWARDS ATONEMENT: MEN, MASCULINITY, AND LOVE

Let me state that i accept personal responsibility for the choices and decisions that i've made in this life, extenuating circumstances notwithstanding. As a man in general and as a conscious New Afrikan man in particular, i think that it's critically important that i take ownership of the choices i've made in this life and the pain i've caused in my community. i think that in order to be genuinely sorry for your actions, you must not only undergo a conscious awakening, but also a spiritual cleansing—not necessarily religious, but a cleansing of your spirit, your very essence and sense of humanity.

In her book *The Will to Change*, bell hooks defines patriarchy as "a political-social system that insists that males are inherently dominating, superior to everything and everyone deemed weak, especially females, and endowed with the right to dominate and rule over the weak and to maintain dominance through various forms of psychological terrorism and violence."[9]

In the same book, hooks quotes psychotherapist John Bradshaw, whose book *Creating Love* gives the dictionary definition of patriarchy as "a social organization marked by the supremacy of the father in the clan or family in both domestic and religious functions." Bradshaw continues: "Patriarchy is characterized by male domination and power . . . patriarchal rules still govern most of the world's religious, school systems and family systems." He lists key points, including "blind obedience—the foundation upon which patriarchy stands: the repression of all emotions except fear; the destruction of individual willpower; and the repression of (critical) thinking whenever it departs from the authority figure's way of thinking."[10]

Our concepts, perceptions, and expressions of sexuality, interpersonal relationships, and social intercourse in general are filtered through this system of patriarchal orientation and domination. If you add the lack of organized political and economic power, along with systemic forms of violence to the mix, the psychosis only intensifies.

Having grown up in prison for most of my life—with my first conviction being a thirty-year sentence at the age of sixteen for attempted robbery—i've lived in hyper-masculine environments where men hide their fears and insecurities behind postures of false bravado or overcompensate by being overly aggressive and hostile. It's an environment where the desire and demand to prove you're a man—dominating, fearless, non-feeling, and non-emotional—becomes so intense that i can't speak to you, acknowledge your humanity, or greet you as a Brother for i fear being perceived as weak. i will stab (or shoot) you, or take your life for a wrong look, a glance, over a debt of thirty-cent ramen noodle soup, or some other perceived slight or disrespect, while the system of political and often criminal power remains intact. It keeps its oppressive foot on Our collective necks and its oppressive feet in Our collective asses!

Just imagine having to live and exist in such an environment day in and day out. Now, imagine the psychological impact, emotional turmoil, and spiritual destruction that such an environment has on one's humanity and psyche. Now, take that and add to it what We see going on in the streets: the vicious cycle of kill, retaliate, kill. When men—suffering from self-hatred and lack of self-knowledge—are taught that, in order to feel secure, they must dominate. All they have left is their perceived "respect," which they will kill (or die) for. And yet, We refuse to kill and destroy the systems of neocolonial oppression, patriarchy, and white supremacy that ensnare Us. We refuse to kill the system that inflicts high unemployment and gentrification upon Our communities, the system that refuses to invest in vital infrastructure, and yet occupies Our communities with law enforcement that has run amok.

During a recent visit with my wife, We had a discussion about what role We wanted to play in the struggle towards social justice if i should get released. i explained to her that, although i was (and We were) tired and just wanted to enjoy life and whatever years We had left on this earth together, i felt the need to explain to her that i had to give back. i had to atone for the pain i'd caused my community, for contributing to the problems that We already collectively faced and struggled against on a daily basis—regardless of whether or not it felt justified at the time. i must stand up and walk through that fire to not only be cleansed, but to serve as an example and beacon of light that might attract others.

Growing up in a capitalist, patriarchal society where Black bodies are routinely commodified, you're desensitized to the value of Black life. From birth, We are indoctrinated by a heavy dose of false concepts that support masculinity, male supremacy, and male privilege. We grow up with a whole warped concept of what it means to be a man (or male). You see, although a lot of Us don't know it, there is a distinction between the two. A lot of Us critique white supremacy because We know what to look for, but We never question male supremacy or male privilege. Oftentimes, We take this area for granted and, as a result, We never move to carry out any type of critical analysis of Our behaviors and the choices We make. Sometimes, We don't even recognize it as a result of social indoctrination. But the choices you're making have already been made for you, and you're just following a script. When you add so-called "race" into the mix, the contradictions only sharpen and intensify.

For New Afrikan men, We have often internalized Our own self-hatred and subjugation to the point that We often seek to destroy those in Our own image. When Black life is devalued and dehumanized, it becomes easier to erase, to hide, to incarcerate, to destroy, and to kill. When you have no answers for your oppression and social reality, your frustration and rage is not only internalized; it explodes into patterns of antisocial and psychopathic behavior.

At some point, some of Us have to be honest with Ourselves— stand up and take ownership of Our choices and actions. i cannot, in good conscience, turn on the news and see what's going on in places like Chicago, listen to the pain and cries of families, watch the funerals of babies hit by stray bullets, and be not only be disgusted, but also self-critical. i question my own history. i cannot be saddened or angry about the loss of friends and associates to heroin or opioid overdoses in these prisons without also critiquing and owning the years of hustling and controlling various economies behind those walls. Awareness and consciousness without personal responsibility is nothing.

How can i pledge allegiance to an organization, or to anything or anyone that was contributing to the killing and murdering of thousands of Us, and not stand up and offer a constructive critique? How can i not take a stance against such? Anyone can kill. That doesn't make Us men—a baby can pull a trigger. In my opinion, men serve and protect their community. We serve, protect, and love Our families and the kids. We love, serve, protect, and struggle beside the womyn in Our lives. Just as We need them to struggle alongside and protect Us. We resist and struggle against Our collective enemies and those who seek to hasten Our demise and destruction.

A body count doesn't make Us men. Being unconscious, unacknowledged serial killers, or spree killers don't make Us men. Being able to hide behind a false sense of bravado and swinging Our dicks doesn't make Us men. My loved ones have been murdered. I've been on the battlefield, on both ends, and I know a lot of Us get caught up in that cycle and are tired. In actuality, We not only want to live, but We also want some peace of mind. Who in their right mind wants to live the way We are forced to live or forced to raise Our children? Yet We have a choice, and the first step is to not only acknowledge Our personal conduct, but to atone for it—repudiate and reject such conduct—and start moving in a different direction.

When my teenage son was murdered, i reverted back to someone i thought i had buried twenty years earlier. You were either with me or against me—with no middle ground. i'm not perfect by a long shot, and i don't pretend to be, but i do know that i have choices. i can make the choice to continue to grow, to evolve, to change, and to be part of the solution, as opposed to continuing to be a part of the problem. What about you?

For me, i have to give back. For me, i have to crawl down in the mud, in the trenches, and try to make a difference. As a conscious New Afrikan man, i have to stand up and be counted. This is the only way i can free and heal myself. It is only through this process that i can genuinely begin to overstand and appreciate the concept of loving thy community as i love thy self. It is only through this self-love, self-critique, and atonement that i can look into the eyes of my daughter and know that she deserves better.

From one generation to the next.

SECTION II:
HISTORY, THEORY, AND PRACTICE

CHAPTER 6

THE NEW AFRIKAN INDEPENDENCE MOVEMENT/ REPUBLIC OF NEW AFRIKA

Land, Independence, and Self-Governance have been objectives sought by Black people ever since We were kidnapped from Afrika and brought to this country as slaves. Many ran away and established communities in the woods, mountains, and swamps. We armed Ourselves and created bases in which We could operate, liberated zones to which other enslaved brothers and sisters might flee. Others organized rebellions, aimed at destroying slavery and liberating territory from which to build an independent state.

To the Black people who were forced to come to this land, Black nationalism was not taken lightly. Although brutally crushed, Our ancestors continued to revolt. Although sold down the river, they continued to escape. Independence and Self-Determination were what they wanted. These Blacks were, in effect, laying bricks on a foundation that was later to become known as the Republic of New Afrika.[11]

The process that gave rise to what became defined as the New Afrikan Nation started on the Afrikan continent and carried over to north amerika. Primarily, the New Afrikan Nation was born as a result of its own internal motion and contradictions. Afrikan tribes were combining into and fused into nations, prior to being transported to amerika.

You may have had one nation comprised of many tribes and, although each tribe had their own distinct tribal identities and culture, they recognized their collective identity based on their particular collective and historical development. For example, the naming of themselves as Angolans, Nigerians, Ghanaians, etc. These are National Distinctions and National Identities. Despite the fact that within their borders they have different tribal origins and relations, their National Identity and National Consciousness are that of a collective definition. Afrikans hold many different theories: some are socialist, some are capitalist, some are nationalist, some are Pan-Afrikanist, and so on. The Republic of New Afrika (RNA) is the name given to the Black Nation in amerika by five hundred nationalist leaders at the Black Government Conference held in Detroit, Michigan, and convened by the Malcolm X Society on March 29–31, 1968. The RNA consists of a population of millions of ideas.

Marcus Garvey once exclaimed, "Where is the [B]lack man's government? Where is his president, his army, his navy, his men of big affairs?"[12]

On March 31, 1968, the seed of Garvey's prophetic vision came to fruition as a force of over five hundred Black nationalists met at the convention in Detroit and issued a Declaration of Independence for a Black nation on the north amerikan continent, named that nation the Republic of New Afrika, and identified five states in the deep south as the subjugated National Territory, creating a basic law and a Provisional Government with elected officials under a mandate to FREE THE LAND!!

THE PROVISIONAL GOVERNMENT TEACHES THAT ALL BLACKS ARE DESCENDANTS OF SLAVES IN NORTH AMERIKA—ARE CITIZENS OF THE REPUBLIC OF NEW AFRIKA BY BIRTH—FOR WE HAD BEEN SNATCHED FROM EVERY REGION IN AFRIKA AND MOLDED BY THIS COMMON HISTORY OF OPPRESSION AND STRUGGLE INTO A NEW AFRIKAN NATION IN THE WORLD.

We were geographically separated from the continent of Afrika, but just as Afrikan as any nation there. Blacks may choose to give up their New Afrikan citizenship, or they may opt for exclusive RNA citizenship. New Afrikan citizenship is a right of birth, and the right to choose in this matter lies at the heart of the New Afrikan Independence Movement. Thus, when the Provisional Government of the Republic of New Afrika (PGRNA) was established, it set about the task of informing Black people of their rights, under international law, to Self-Determination, Land, and Reparations. Since its existence, the PGRNA has sharpened the theoretical basis for New

Afrikan Political Science, organized national elections for government officials, demanded reparations from the u.s. state, defended itself against enemy attacks, sought to establish diplomatic relations with other governments, and struggled for the rights of New Afrikan Prisoners of War. Freedom, Self-Government, and Self-Determination—the objectives sought by Blacks since Our arrival on these shores—had now reached a higher stage.[13]

The "Movement" to "Free the Land"

It is important to note that the PGRNA was established by New Afrikans who held a number of different political, economic, and social theories. Those who founded the PGRNA collectively recognized that an Afrikan (Black) Nation in amerika does exist. They named it New Afrika, created the Provisional Government for it, and gave the PG the dual mission of educating the New Afrikan masses with regard to Our true National Identity and of struggling for Independence in the states of Mississippi, Alabama, Georgia, South Carolina, and Louisiana. These states are part of the historical Black Belt birthplace and the north amerikan farmland of the New Afrikan Nation. This area is called the New Afrikan National Territory.

The struggle to free this land is called the NAIM. All those in the movement recognize the existence of the nation and partake in the struggle to free it.

While there is a clarion call to "Free The Land" and a movement to target these particular states that We identify as Our National Territory, nothing is exempt from undergoing change and evolution. We also know that, while there may be a dialectical-materialist and theoretical basis to support the establishment of a Sovereign/Independent National Territory, some realities will be decided by boots on the ground: through the motion of the people, of the masses. Any serious struggle or war for the National Liberation of New Afrikan People and for Socialism will not leave the continental north amerikan continent as We know it. Any form of people's war in the u.s. by the masses for the establishment of a socialist or communist entity will cause a total reconfiguration of the u.s. empire as We know it.

Various elements, groups, and people who profess to be allies try to deny the legitimacy of Our right to wage a National Liberation Struggle or a Struggle for Self-Determination. As such, these allies often reek of settler arrogance, paternalism, hidden agendas, and thinly-camouflaged white nationalism. These superficial allies have never done any real research or investigation into the historical development of the New Afrikan Nation or the history and origin of the New Afrikan Independence Movement. We do not need or seek your validation.

The rhythm of a people never stops, whether they are transported across oceans, in the bowels of slave ships, or if they remain stationary. That beat and culture continues, advancing along its path of development and evolution, shaped and conditioned by its current conditions and objective material reality. With that being said, the residue of the old remains as it contributes and gives rise to and helps to form and shape the new.

Our Struggle for Land, Independence, and Socialism is no less valid or less legitimate than the anti-colonial wars waged on the continent of Afrika to oust the portuguese, the british, the belgian, and other settlers.

In fact, since the arrival of Our ancestors on these shores, We have continuously waged a war for Land and Independence from the settler, colonizing, and imperialist u.s. government. Whether it was in the form of maroons fighting the colonial british forces to a standstill; whether it was forcing the u.s. colonial forces to sign peace treaties or ceasefire treaties as We retreated into the hills and/or swamps with indigenous allies; whether it is screaming in the streets that "Black Lives Matter" as We rebelled and revolted in the urban ghetto colonies across amerika; whether it was as We launched raiding parties from the swamps and hills to attack and set fire to slave plantations.

This was war and, despite the fact that second-class citizenship was imposed upon Us with the Thirteenth and Fourteenth Amendments—changing chattel slavery from private individual ownership to that of state ownership—this war against neocolonialism and genocide has not stopped or ceased; it has merely taken on various forms as it goes through its stages of development and dialectical processes. You do not amend a people into a constitution. You do not get to impose second-class citizenship upon a conquered or colonized people. In fact, it is a violation of international law as defined by the United Nations regarding formally conquered or colonized people.

Article Fifteen of the Universal Declaration of Human Rights, a founding document of the United Nations passed in 1948, has two points:

1) Everyone has a right to a nationality.
2) No one shall be arbitrarily deprived of his nationality nor denied the right to change his nationality.[14]

When people talk about it being "two amerikas," when people talk about the rate of imprisonment of New Afrikan people, the rate that New Afrikan people are murdered by colonial occupational personnel (cops), or when We talk about the rate of Black womyn dying from various forms of cancer, the school-to-prison pipeline for Our children, the environmental racism pumping poisonous water into Our schools and communities, etc., this represents national oppression and genocide. It ain't never been no "one amerika" except white racist-settler amerika, so to say "two amerikas" is a misnomer. It is an attempt to divert a proper political assessment and analysis from the truth and prevent Us from going down a path that doesn't lead to National liberation or freedom. It is a strategic and a military diversionary tactic designed to keep Us away from more militant forms of struggle and resistance.

The New Afrikan Liberation Collective represents just one of the many organizations within the NAIM.[15] We invite you to unite with Us as We struggle to not only Free The Land but build up and strengthen the Provisional Government of the Republic of New Afrika and advance Our *Vita Wa Watu*! FREE THE LAND![16]

Postscript

For additional information pertinent to the argument articulated in this article, see 1) Articles II and III of the UN's International Convention on the Punishment of the Crime of Genocide; 2) the Programme of Action for the Full Implementation of the Declaration on the Granting of Independence to Colonial Countries and Peoples; and 3) the International Covenant on Economic, Social, and Cultural Rights.[17] Article II in the UN's 's International Convention on the Punishment of the Crime of Genocide reads: "In the present Convention, genocide means any of the following acts committed with intent to destroy, in whole or in part, a national, ethnical, racial, or religious group, as such:

> (a) Killing members of the group; (b) Causing serious bodily or mental harm to members of the group; (c) Deliberately inflicting on the group conditions of life calculated to bring about its physical destruction in whole or in part; (d) Imposing measures intended to prevent births within the group; (e) Forcibly transferring children of the group to another group."

Next, Article III in the same Convention establishes the specific crimes penalized by the parties of the Convention, reads that the following acts shall be punishable:

> (a) Genocide; (b) Conspiracy to commit genocide; (c) Direct and public incitement to commit genocide; (d) Attempt to commit genocide; (e) Complicity in genocide.[18]

In 1970, the UN General Assembly adopted Resolution 2621 on implementing the prior declaration of the right of colonized peoples to Self-Determination, noting that

> Colonial peoples have the inherent right to struggle by all necessary means at their disposal against colonial Powers which suppress their aspirations for freedom and independence.

Finally, the very first article of the first part of the International Covenant on Civil and Political Rights and International Covenant on Economic, Social, and Cultural Rights, adopted by the UN General Assembly in 1966 stated again that:

> All people have the right of self-determination. By virtue of that right they freely determine their political status and freely pursue their economic, social, and cultural development.

CHAPTER 7
AN HONEST CONVERSATION AND SELF-CRITIQUE

There can be no honest conversation about whether Black Lives Matter (BLM) without including the voices of the hundreds of thousands of Black men and womyn behind the iron curtain of the prison walls.[19] There can be no honest conversation about BLM without an honest critique and psychosocial analysis of the civil wars—i.e. gang wars, Black-on-Black violence, and the murder rate that—are out of control in Our community.

While We reject the right-wing conservative and generally backwards apologist positions that attempt to use Black-on-Black violence as a justification or rationalization for state-sanctioned violence at the hands of its security forces (i.e. police or privileged white males who have a license to kill and murder Black folks based on their skin privilege of being identified as white), there must be an honest assessment, analysis, and solution-oriented approach.

While We know that street-level violence is a direct result of state-level violence, the policies of u.s. government—regardless of the "party" in power or the administration—feed this violence through the inequality of resource distribution to communities of color and in urban areas; the disproportionate over-incarceration; saturation policing (for all the good it does); and a lack of jobs. These conditions directly contribute to what is raging in Our communities, which often manifest as civil wars driven by the drug economy and economics in general. It is a vicious cycle motivated and sponsored by state and racist-sanctioned genocide.

You cannot close schools, hospitals, and clinics and have no jobs and not expect or anticipate the explosion of violence. You cannot put rats in a cage, in a controlled environment of behavioral modification, reward them and punish them, and overall, environmentally manipulate them as they will, eventually, begin to feed upon one another. While We are far from rodents to be exterminated—at the hands of the state and its governmental policies—We have to seize Our own destiny and give guidance to Our future generations.

When forgiving Our proven enemies becomes more important than demanding justice and organizing for real freedom, we have a flawed and defective stereotype. When it becomes more important than organizing Ourselves from the bottom up to defend and protect Ourselves from those that ravish and murder Us from outside of Our community, as well as those backward elements (of which I Used to be one of) within Our community and among Us, then We have to reassess Our strategy for survival. We are one of the only people on the planet who can be lynched, mass murdered, mass incarcerated, and subjected to apartheid-type policies and governing, yet still bend over backwards to forgive and make peace. Fuck that!! It is not a crime to organize in order to protect yourself—to survive. Armed self-defense isn't a crime. To patrol and control your own community isn't a crime. To fight for human survival is a human right. Singing "We Shall Overcome" while being marched into ovens or prisons is ludicrous!!!

Does anyone have a problem with white males patrolling (and exercising white male privilege) in the streets of Ferguson with semi-automatic weapons and tactical gear? i'm talking about so-called white "civilians"/citizens. Not only were they patrolling, but freely interacting with the state security forces (police) and engaging in coordinated tactical maneuvers. Why isn't anyone talking about this? Where is the outrage? This was being done under the guise of so called "Oath Keepers" protecting the people from the state. Can you imagine Black men walking not only the streets of Ferguson with semi-automatic rifles—let alone a predominantly white area—and it not resulting in an armed confrontation with the police or other armed agents? It isn't safe for Us to, legally, walk around armed in an open-carry state—let alone an open warzone. Open apartheid in occupied Azania (South Afrika) wasn't that long ago.

The civil wars that broke out in the former Federal People's Republic of Yugoslavia—in Bosnia, Herzegovina, and Kosovo—Rwanda, and Burundi, weren't that long ago. These were civil wars dictated by racial and religious hatred, manipulated and controlled by state and government forces and u.s. imperialism and neocolonialism.

While We know and *overstand* that the BLM movement was created to focus on white cops killing Black people and exposing such, We also recognize that the movement isn't monolithic. Some groups are also using the strategy and tactic of leaderless resistance. Can genocidal oppression truly be reformed?

Yeah, Black lives matter. While demanding that you recognize such, one has to *overstand* that wars—called low-intensity wars—are raging in this country. It's imperative that We organize for survival. We have people not only walking into Our churches and killing Our people but burning them down!!!

Whatever God (or not) you believe in, when you're not even safe in a house of worship or sacred space, when people don't see you as human . . . how can We forgive and rationalize such sickness and hatred?

This isn't about good cop or bad cop. Our people all over amerika and in Our community have a distinctive and oppressive relationship to the state and its security forces (i.e. the police).

The police represent an institution and an organization based upon ideology and operating procedures. This relationship has always been oppressive, both historically and up until one second ago. These people and institutions have never represented Us or Our collective interest. It doesn't matter if you have a "Black" president or attorney general. How is it that in most of Our communities, which are patrolled heavier than any other, We can have any acronym one can think of (e.g., FBI, DEA, ATF, JTTF, etc.) and one still can't decrease the murder rate, or stop and facilitate the removal and replacement of the drug economy in Our neighborhoods? Why are they really there? And, more importantly, whose interests are they operating under? Because it shows it ain't Our damn interest. This is why We can't depend on them or their government and why it begins with Us utilizing the practice and concept of dual power, allowing Us to operate utilizing Our own resources to build and create Our own institutions.

The contradictions and dialectics We see playing out in society also manifest themselves inside of amerika's prisons—behind the iron

curtain of barbed wire, surveillance gear, gun towers, and genocide—
under the guise of corrections. What are they correcting when all
they are doing is warehousing Us and brutalizing Us? The wholesale
manufacturing of psycho-sociopaths that are released upon Our community—creating people full of rage, depression, and PTSD issues.
You torture, abuse, and then cut funding and remove mental health
services from Our community!!! A hidden agenda . . .

You do not "correct" by cutting programs in the prisons. You
do not "correct" by removing the vocational trades and training to
the point of no real jobs or mental health intervention for Us—only
giving hours on end locked in cages, where solitary confinement
becomes a solution to a lack of bed space. So again, whose interest are
these places serving, while private prisons and investments in such are
booming? Just ask Michael Jordan!

If Black lives matter, they matter on all fronts. We are a nation
of people. You can call it Black amerika or whatever, but We are a
nation, with a separate and distinct relationship to amerika, its settler
agents, and its representatives. We are of you, and shall at some point,
return to you. We must be a part of the BLM conversation and its
transitioning.

The New Afrikan Liberation Collective in Indiana represents only
one aspect of this conversation. PPs and socially-conscious prisoners
are not only seizing the time and opportunity to organize amongst
Ourselves, but are also being heard. From a whisper to a shout, to a
scream—Our lives matter too!!!!

From one generation to the next, on behalf of the New Afrikan
Liberation Collective (NALC).

CHAPTER 8

TACTICS AND STRATEGIES IN THE STRUGGLE FOR INDEPENDENCE: QUESTIONS FOR CONTINUED REFLECTION

Introduction

When you study revolutions in general and "third world" revolutions in particular, people who are fighting to overthrow or remove the yoke of colonial or imperial oppression/domination, you see a "rebirth" of consciousness, a "coming out of the self" through the revolutionary process.[20] Part of the struggle for liberation is also the struggle to not only Free the Land, to Free the Nation, but also the struggle to define who We are and what We are and establish for Ourselves, Our collective identify based on Our historical development. That is a part of the right to Self-Determination as opposed to being branded. As opposed to having an identity such as Negro, nigger, Black, or African American imposed upon you by some celebrity or other illegitimate authoritative figure that isn't based upon material fact.

Fact and Fiction: The Right to Self-Determination of the Oppressed

Often Our struggle for Independence, for New Afrikan liberation and Self-Determination is equated with white separation or white supremacy. Particularly euro-amerikans often try to equate the Black Panther Party or any New Afrikan nationalist, socialist, or revolutionary organization with being Black supremacist which is a false contrast not rooted in historical or materialist fact. First of all, We hate and are opposed to any form of oppression and We are opposed to any oppressive power structure that denies people their human rights for whatever reason. Second, New Afrikans do not and have never had the power base, infrastructure, or government structure to systematically target euro-amerikans for disenfranchisement, lynchings, or any other forms of violent oppression, political or otherwise, nor have their ever been a new Afrikan political or radical organization that as part of the black supremacist political platform who went around the country targeting or terrorizing euro-amerikans in Our attempt to keep them enslaved, disenfranchised, or under yoke of New Afrikan domination.

In fact, and in contrast, when you look at the history of such groups as the Klan, White Citizens' Councils, etc., these groups were often made up of pillars of the white community, the local law enforcement, the property owners, the businessmen, schoolteachers, clergy, farmers, politicians, etc. In essence the very power structure of white amerika and its settler population were either directly a member of these groups or acted as auxiliary shock troops when it came time to oppress, control, lynch, or disenfranchise new amerika, Native indigenous people, Mexicans, etc., both as an oppressed people as a whole, as well as individuals. In contrast show me one New Afrikan group/organization that has/had the same power and the same politics. You can't! So, stop lying! You cannot equate Our reaction to racism, to genocide, to viciousness perpetrated by euro-amerika and its power structure and try to label Us.

We have a right to be enraged. We have a right on some levels to hate. It's what you choose to do with that rage and hate and whether or not you choose to channel it toward something good and productive. For Us, liberation is both good & productive. We have the right to self-defense. All over the world the u.s. bombed and waged war against oppressed people but tell Us to be positive and to sing, pray, forgive, and all of that. The united states government sells more weapons on the arms market than any other country in the world. Yet tell communities of color to disarm, that We shouldn't want, have, or train with firearms while the white community even down to its children buy, stockpile, and train with firearms by the dozens. Black-on-Black violence in Our communities is a byproduct of state-sanctioned white-on-Black violence and the subjugation and disenfranchisement of New Afrikan people. The oppressive and genocidal government policies and unequal distribution and concentration of wealth both inflicted and perpetuated by this government are the primary contributing factors to the violence.

On the Question of Multinational Unity

There must be honest conversation about so called race, class, and genocide. amerika refuses to hear the complaints and criticism by the New Afrikan people unless We disremember Our story and only remember history, unless We renounce Our blackness under the pretense and white-washed concept of "we are all amerikans." You see people reject and fear the concept "Black Lives Matter" unless the dominant eurocentric culture gets to control the narrative or unless it is corralled into a safe space and corridor of amerikanism. Have you ever thought what the criteria for becoming an amerikan is? Surely just being born isn't sufficient because, if it were you, wouldn't need all these civil right acts, amendments, and other pieces of paper that don't mean anything. euro-amerikans claim to feel oppressed like a second-class citizen in their own country. Why? Because people are saying you're no longer going to be allowed to dictate and dominate, and control all the resources just because you're a euro-amerikan? Why? Because white lives are the only lives that matter and within the next twenty to twenty-five years you will be considered a national settler minority and you fear this new reality? Thus, you seek a desperate Hitlerian final solution. This is why a Donald Trump type can sound so musical to your tone-deaf ears.

We know that there are euro-amerikans and working-class people who are poor and impoverished, who are being screwed over by the ruling capitalist elites, and who, like Us, want a better quality of life for their children and families. But the question is this: Are you willing to join the revolution to achieve a better quality of life, or are you going to align yourself with the u.s. police state and neofascism so that so that your quality of life improves while that of others—people of color in particular—continues to deteriorate? While people of color continue to be mass-incarcerated and shot in the back by neo-colonial occupational personnel (cops)? While New Afrikans suffer double-digit unemployment and the highest infant mortality rate? What side of history will you stand on?

From Protest to Resistance

How do We move from protest to actual resistance? How do We invade public and private space and serve notice that there can no longer be any business as usual, there can be no peace or so-called democracy with racist oppression, inequality, neocolonial, imperialist domination, and genocide? A strategy has to be articulated that is multi-pronged. Protest alone is just emotionalism. It's not going to move Us forward. Protest has to be tied into a larger strategy seeking concrete goals and objectives. For example, now that a lot of "Us" have regurgitated the Obama Kool-Aid and the smoke-and-mirror mirage of hope and change has vaporized and reality has set in, how do We move towards exposing and calling to task a lot of these positive neo-liberal house slaves to task for not representing Our collective interest? We should move to force policy changes, legislative changes, by putting forth Our agendas through mass action and mass organizing and by refusing to allow the establishment negro social fireman/fire-woman to come in, seek out concerns, and try to extinguish righteous rage and voices of the people, especially the voices of the youth.

We need to launch a grassroot campaign to mobilize Our communities, especially the youth and college students, to move beyond the safe zone of liberal politics and actually create institutions that cater to the needs of Our people and communities. We need to engage with a more radical, critical consciousness while striving to pool Our resources and build Our own social infrastructure, thereby becoming self-empowering. We need to move towards a strategy of self-defense and offense. There has to be accountability and consequences when those that represent power murder Us. There has to be political, economic, and personal consequences and accountability when racist or terroristic colonial occupational personal and or individuals murder Us in the streets, jails, and prisons. The federal government can't police the police; the Department of Justice (DOJ)—with all of its lame investigations—ain't going to save Us. We need to learn how to more effectively strip away the legitimacy of the state and expose the government for what it is. A constructive strategy has to be developed that addresses and deals with the rage and self-hatred that exists among Us, the rage that feeds the so-called Black-on-Black violence and homicide rate in Our community. How do We harness this anger and rage and give it proper constructive direction? How do We learn to know thyself as We know the enemy?

The act of resistance is a lot different from just protesting. When you resist, you're no longer just screaming the liberal slogan of "no justice, no peace." Instead, you have a specific strategy, utilizing a specific set of tactics to obtain specific goals and objectives. When you resist, you're playing both offense and defense. In this context We want to fight for Self-Determination, fight for the right to determine the quality of Our lives, and fight to be free from continued imperialist racist domination and oppression.

When you have people say We must take this country back, We must make amerika great again, what do you think they mean? "We can't let them have Our country; We need to bring back the good old days (niggers knew their place)." The country/empire is headed towards and authoritarian, militarized, police state and the issue of so-called "race," i.e. neocolonial oppression, is going to be the main attraction, the central theme park. We are Our own liberators, no one is going to save you/us. We have to think in terms of survival.

For those behind the prison walls, Our voices must be collectively raised as We strive to build principled relationships and coalitions across the lines of superficial divisions. Some of Us are going to die behind these lines. For some of Us with these fifty, sixty, and life sentences, there ain't no getting out. It's just Us and therefore We have to fight, struggle, and sacrifice to force changes for the future generations, for Our sons and daughters, who risk the same fate as Us, or worse.

Prisons merely represent just another front in the struggle for liberation of oppressed people. The only difference is We are trapped behind enemy lines. We still have a role to play and contribution. How can i educate myself and others? How can i improve my conditions and reality? How can i add my voice to the chorus of millions screaming for freedom or death? How can i expose and put a stop to the racist beatings and murders by and vicious brutality of so-called correctional officers (who ain't correcting a damn thing) and prison rats, and in the process firmly establish in word and in deed that such acts will no longer be passively tolerated/accepted? That there are consequences for murdering the Sandra Blands of the world. How can We demand the tools and programs that improve the quality of Our lives and improve the chances of those who do get released someday? And most of all, how do We move to become less dependent upon the state and instead take personal responsibility, to become self-reliant and independent in order to move in a positive, self-affirming direction and utilize Our own collective and individual genius to create Our own life sustaining programs, infrastructure, and institution?

In closing, let me leave you with this thought. When the Declaration of Independence and Constitution were written, We as a people were not even considered human. We were considered three-fifths of a human being. Later, according to the u.s. Supreme Court in the Dred Scott ruling, "A black man had no rights that a white man was bound to respect." You don't amend a people into a constitution. You don't impose a constitution upon a conquered or enslaved people and call it freedom!! When you amend or insert the Voting Rights Act, the Civil Rights Act, and all the other acts that the ruling elites act like don't exist, they can just as easily be repealed, be removed. All across the land you see the powers that be changing the rules of the game as soon as you learn how to play the game or think you're winning. We are witnessing new forms of voter suppression, redistricting, new poll taxes, etc. This whole charade is like Three-card Monte: every time you know which card the pea is under, they shuffle the cards again and it doesn't matter if it's the republicans, democrats, or congressional Black caucus—history has repeatedly proven that it is all smoke and mirrors, and that they and therefore today's reality not only dictate but issue the mandate that the only solution is to turn over the whole table that the game is being played on.

Which side will you stand on?

CHAPTER 9

THE CONCEPT AND PRACTICE OF DUAL POWER: THE OPPORTUNITY TO REBUILD A MOVEMENT

One concept of revolutionary dual power is the application of political theory and ideology to concrete conditions. This concept is applicable to mass organizing work, prison solidarity work, and similar efforts. In this instance, i would like to discuss some of the responses and work being done in response to this COVID-19 attack. Specifically, the work that is being done by revolutionary, radical, militant, or progressive groups and organizations in various communities throughout the empire.

When the COVID-19 attack hit, everyone was fearful and nervous because We weren't entirely sure what it was. Some self-interested groups and media outlets hyped and manipulated that fear—some for self-serving interests, some for capitalist economic reasons, and others just out of ignorance.

You see, when it comes to one another, it's easy to fear what you don't know or understand. Decades of social conditioning through movies like *Mad Max, The Purge*, and *Isaiah* have conditioned some of Us to instinctively fear Our neighbors; it manifests through hoarding food, stockpiling weapons, or going online to fan the flames of this fear.

Then there are those like Us—people who believe in, fight for, and struggle for a better future. We fight for a more just and humane world, free of all the negative "isms" that destroy people and entire generations: racism, capitalism, colonialism, and imperialism, which suck the life out of Us all; sexism and homophobia, which create and perpetuate sexual and social violence in Our communities.

Dual power is the practice of not depending on the government to meet the needs of the people and the community. Dual power means rebuilding parallel structures and infrastructures that serve the needs of the people—all people. In actuality, dual power functions as a parallel government, empowering the people to do for themselves and utilize their resources to meet the needs of their community.

We serve the people and their interests because their interests are Our interests. We organize, network, and empower the people to take control and responsibility for their own destiny.

Indiana Organizing as an Example

How do We do that?

In Indiana, groups and organizations like Indiana Department of Corrections (IDOC) Watch, the New Afrikan Liberation Collective (NALC), the NABPP, various BLM chapters, and many others are deeply rooted in the community. They organize food drives and set up distribution networks for critical resources like clothes and medications. They establish taxi-type services for people who don't have transportation, come to understandings with street organizations, and work alongside the New Afrikan Black Panther Party to implement security networks and patrols in Our neighborhoods. These efforts allow Us to avoid relying on or having the state police and national guards' involvement. Some collectives have also started community gardens, distributing the food to people and families in need. All of this is being done freely.

We don't care about so-called "race," gender, or any category you are; We care about serving the people and setting the example of socialism in both theory and practice.

In Indiana, We also took the lead—along with many comrades in other states—in calling for and demanding the release of prisoners who were either at risk or had a year or less left on their sentences.

Prisoners' families contacted Us, and We utilized various forms of social media to organize and cultivate working relationships with people from diverse backgrounds and walks of life. What did We have in common? Our care for someone locked down in these modern-day concentration camps. We cared about prisoners/captives, about how the state and government disregard Our/their lives. We organized phone zaps targeting various seats of power, demanding the release of prisoners. People organized protests and rallies in front of jails and prisons and held press conferences. In solidarity, prisoners in at least three other prisons went on mass hunger strikes, demanding basic humane treatment, to be issued face masks, to have access to testing, to not be punished with solitary confinement for developing symptoms.

By working with Our outside comrades, going into churches, and activating Our own distribution networks, We have both learned from the people and exposed them to Our politics and vision. What We see developing on the ground in Indiana, and behind enemy lines, is a result of the work that groups and collectives like IDOC Watch, New Afrikan Liberation Collective, Black Lives Matters, and Prison Lives Matter have been doing for years in the state, with boots on the ground.

With this growing momentum and more people seeking to get involved, and as the sleeping giant behind prison walls continues to awaken, We must seize the moment.

The media wants to highlight the little, cute, "feel-good" social networking being done online—viral videos, Tik Tok trends, and mass social interactions. While these have their place, We have a vision for a new society. We believe in the radical transformation of society: a society where prisons and caging people are no longer necessary, where elders aren't neglected and abandoned in underfunded, profit-driven nursing homes, institutions, businesses, or corporations, and a world no longer structured by class. We want an end to this society where privileged folks get health care, testing, and treatment, while poor folks are left with death! We want an end to a world where We get mass graves, or bodies left unclaimed or in unrefrigerated U-Haul Trucks on the streets of Brooklyn, NY!

People are always saying "that can't happen in amerika." This is real and it's happening. The lack of government resources distributed to hospitals, poor communities, or rural areas is a glimpse of the future.

Dual power allows Us to prepare for these realities. It enables Us to build the political, economic, and military structures necessary to realize a better world. It gives Us the opportunity to share, discuss, and break down Our politics, overcoming the superficialities that separate Us as We learn, teach, and grow. Sometimes, breaking the rules is necessary to create new ones that work for everyone and are applied equally.

We have teachers, nurses, medical professionals, engineers, and people with other skills among Us. Plus, a lot of people who have lost their jobs, people who didn't (or don't) have savings, and people who are hurting. These people also need help. Our comrades are purchasing land and properties for community centers. Why not extend this by establishing community seizure of empty lots to plant community gardens for community consumption?

When contradictions sharpen between Us and the state, and they attempt to criminalize Us, spread propaganda against Us, and isolate or neutralize Us, it will be the masses We serve who will stand with Us, fight for Us, and protect Us.

This is why, when workers at Amazon, Walmart, and other companies walk off the job in protest over unsafe working conditions, We should be there to give support, to follow their lead in demanding these companies or government entities be held accountable. We also must try to meet their needs where possible.

In Indiana, We have the opportunity to build and strengthen the movement. We also have the chance to push the state to make concessions regarding its so-called criminal justice system. It's time for Indiana to catch up with the twenty-first century and how to treat its prisoners, with how it sentences its so-called citizens, and with its lack of parole boards or chance for early release. Indiana's new sentencing guidelines forced the rate of incarceration up another 35 percent. It's time for these people to be challenged, exposed, and held accountable.

For activist groups with no history or experience in doing prisoner solidarity work, you should form prisoner solidarity committees within your own groups and organizations (so that you can research and discuss amongst yourselves). i would suggest that you try to develop working relationships with other groups who have already done, or are actively doing, some of this work—groups that have working relationships with the prisoners that they claim to represent. i would suggest you try to develop a principled, working relationship with a PP, an activist prisoner, or a progressive prison group. We can further build this movement by establishing points of unity, areas, and issues We agree on and try to build a coalition. A coalition where We leave egos and petty differences at the door. Maybe We can develop a statewide Steering Committee, maybe a Coalition of Delegates, and try to build a solid movement and sustain Our momentum.

Remember: dual power helps Us to build and put in place the basic infrastructure and pillars of the society We seek to create. It also helps Us heal and recover from the damage caused by living under this system, while simultaneously working to dismantle the sick social intercourse and relations—like racism—We've been taught to think are so natural.

All Power to the People!!
Free All Political Prisoners!!

CHAPTER 10

PRISON ABOLITIONISM: TAILORING THE MESSAGE

Introduction

When an entity or organization like the DOC is a law unto itself, there exists no checks or balances, and, consequently, no accountability. Thus, it is left up to the people—to the masses—to hold them accountable and to regulate those whom the DOC professes to represent and proclaims to govern!

Ego-Defense Mechanisms

The following three paragraphs are quoted from *Black-on-Black Violence* by Amos Wilson:

> Denial and distortion are the classical categorical means commonly referred to as ego defense mechanisms, by which an ego complex avoids unpleasant confrontations with reality itself and its own pathological history and current functioning. Through denial and distortion of reality and its concomitant self-deception, the collective white american ego complex rationalizes and repressively ignores its origination and sustenance by means of its enslavement, rape, robbery, and murder of captive peoples; its ruthless unconscionable wasteful and toxic exploitation of the land, labor, and resources of other peoples; its unwarranted wars against other nations and

cultures, its exploitative instigation of wars among them; its duplicitous diplomacy and propaganda, treachery and deceit, war mongering and invitations to riot; its colonizing, neo-colonizing, terrorizing, starvation, benign and malicious neglect, usurious taxation of captive populations; its segregation, discriminations, dehumanizations, psych manipulations of other peoples and nations in flagrant violation of its own vaunted moral preachments; its closing of its ears to the cries of its victims, sclerotic hardening of its psychic arteries.

By means of defensive denial and distortion, self-deception and reversal of reality, the collective eurocentric ego complex seeks to resolve itself by creating conflicts and contradictions, to avoid feelings of guilt, shame and anxiety, to neutralize and negate self-perceptions, and to protect its material advantages. To these ends its victims must be blamed for their own victimization. Their suffering must be seen as reflections of their own inherent deficiencies, of their servile manifest destiny, and of their being shortchanged by God and Fate.

Societal amnesia, a society's repression of the memory of the traumatic experiences which created its structure and character, is markedly typical of the collective white American ego complex. The domination of African Americans is made all the more effective and comforting to the collective white American ego if its historical and current dominative processes are kept from its own consciousness and the consciousness of the subordinate African American community. Historically embarrassing behavior, lowly and criminal origins, revelations of social iniquities and their progeny, hidden from consciousness, permits the myth of the inherent moral, social, cultural, intellectual superiority of the white American complex to persist unchallenged and enhances the efficiency of its exploitation of Africans at home and abroad.[21]

This is the bubble in which the amerikan criminal justice system exists and conducts its daily operations. The attempt to isolate and separate the criminal justice system and "law enforcement" from its historical origins and context doesn't stand up to mental reasoning or critique.

Study after study has shown that in most so-called urban inner-city areas, such as various boroughs in New York or counties throughout the state of Indiana that have a high concentration of Black and Brown people, there are the highest rates of arrest, conviction, and incarceration. In contrast, white "suspects" or people arrested for similar or identical offenses (if arrested at all) do not receive the same treatment or application of the law.

This isn't a coincidence and can't be separated from the historical continuity of colonization and white supremacy that have contaminated and infected the very core of the u.s. and its institutions, as well as its various branches of government—legislative, executive, and judicial.

We have heard politician after politician, academics, think tanks, etc. critique the dysfunctionality and racist application of the laws and punishment in this society. It's interesting that former presidents Barack Obama, Bill Clinton, and Hillary Clinton, all came out and stated that the "crime bill," signed by Bill Clinton, had a negative and racial social impact on the New Afrikan community. This bill hampered prisoners' ability to file civil suits on their behalf, to file habeas corpus appeals challenging their convictions, or to hold the state and federal governments accountable. Yet nothing has been corrected about it other than the window dressing and band-aid approach of making up the discrepancy between powder and crack cocaine. What about the thousands upon thousands of generational youth and young New Afrikan men and womyn that were railroaded into the PIC, especially during the era of the so-called War on Drugs?

This is why We believe in Prison Abolition. We do not believe that the PIC, especially as a billion-dollar industry, can be reformed. Just as We don't believe that capitalism as a socioeconomic system can be reformed so that it can be just in its application to all peoples of society.

People hear Us speak about Prison Abolition or Defunding the Police and have a certain perception or image that isn't always accurate.

For those of Us, specifically those who are of an oppressed class or an oppressed Nation of people, We believe in and envision a society where there neither exists nor is a need for prisons. A society where there is not a need to cage people primarily as a result of the unequal distribution of wealth or equal access to resources. We envision a society where there doesn't exist a class structure, where the lower classes get dumped on by the higher classes or ruling elites and/or privilege or institutionalized racism and neocolonialism is used to both rationalize and justify and/or justify such.

Tailoring the Message

We believe that activists, revolutionaries, and prison abolitionists must tailor this message to fit into the social reality of the ghetto colonies of amerika if We are in fact trying to politicize, organize, and help facilitate empowering these communities.

What does prison abolition mean in real time to someone that lives in a community where rampant crime, daily sex offenses, murders, warlordism, and reactionary violence exist? They aren't trying to hear nothing about Prison Abolition or defunding the police! The concept doesn't have a positive impact on their/Our lives or alter Our daily reality. We can't suggest to grandma not to call the police when her home is robbed by the local addict or whatever if you're not willing to go into that community and organize so that:

1) There is no need for anyone to rob grandma or
2) They can come up with their own rules, laws, policies, and enforcement/accountability.

A community organized, taught, and trained to defend itself against those reactionary elements within and against oppressive government forces from without.

We don't always have to use language that has been so stigmatized by the power structure where people instantly have a negative reaction if they hear words like anarchy, socialism, communalism, etc. Sometimes it helps to break it down far as the actual benefits and practice or nature of such.

Sometimes it's not just about screaming racism, although that might actually be what it is. Sometimes it's about showing people concretely how this or that impacts Us, and why and how We can change it. It's about explaining that prisons haven't always existed, who actually socially/economically benefits from prisons, and the origins and intended social role of so-called amerikan law enforcement. More importantly, it's about showing how the people can empower themselves to govern themselves.

For example, during a lot of natural disasters, or the height of the COVID-19 pandemic, people came together, organized, and helped thy neighbors. People who ordinarily might not even speak to one another found ways to connect with each other in solidarity. The powers that be want Us divided so that We can't unify and focus on them.

Human Rights Violations

Contrary to popular propaganda, amerika isn't this beacon of light on the hill that doesn't house PPs, POWs, or Political Dissenters within its jails. It is just like any other empire: it interns and criminalizes and incarcerates its critics and revolutionaries that the government deems a threat to its power base or status quo. The u.s. government routinely violates the United Nations Standard Minimum Rules for the Treatment of Prisoners, also known as "The Nelson Mandela Rules."[22] The u.s. prison system and its prisoncrats routinely target, torture, abuse, and occasionally murder those Prisoners of War (POW), Prison Activists, and Jailhouse Lawyers, either murder outright or through years of medical neglect or misdiagnosis. Again, in violation of the UN Charter on Human Rights.

We are routinely held in supermax prisons or solitary confinement where We are trapped in a cell for twenty-three hours a day. This is often with done to those with exemplary prison conduct records, who do not engage in acts of violence unless necessary (and sometimes it is necessary to defend Ourselves or beat back the rabid dogs that kill and maim Us under the color of law). We are targeted for being politically active. Within the PIC, you can lose your life for fighting for your rights, or for educating and/or organizing other prisoners. For such, the thought police will attack you, outsource your demise to more reactionary and less woke elements, isolate you, extend your prison sentence, and ship you off to a different state into domestic exile.

i appeal to the common person who says they believe in the rule of law. Do you believe in supporting unjust laws or the unjust or unequal application of such laws? i appeal to those who say they support human rights. i appeal to those who criticize China, Iran,

Cuba, and other countries for alleged human rights abuses but say and do nothing about the abuses taking place in the prisons in your state, city, or neighborhood.

Don't say you believe in God, but sanction and turn a blind eye to the work of the devil?

If you protest and attack someone who might have been convicted of a sex offense or a murder, who has served his/her sentence, and run them out of your community just because you can do so, will you allow a prison guard who beats and tortures handcuffed prisoners, who spits in prisoners' food, who might belong to a white supremacist organization, who will search Our cells and, out of spite, destroy personal photos of Our children, to live freely in your community without fear of neither criticism, ridicule, nor accountability? Will you allow this person to coach little league teams, teach your children, and live a "normal" existence when, in fact, everything about their personality and social behavior is abnormal? The height or epitome of hypocrisy!!!

If someone worked in a Nazi death camp and had been killing, exterminating people all day, wouldn't you consider it abnormal for this person to be able to immerse himself back into a community, have dinner with his family, play with his children? Would you consider it acceptable for them to shuck it off as "just another day at the office!!?" Ahh, "i left that at work, i don't bring my job home with me." Really??

On December 21, 2021, following my transfer from Green Rock Correctional Center by Sgt. B.L. Towler (against whom i had a pending grievance and criminal complaint), was the victim of a hate crime upon my arrival at River North Correctional Center. From the very point of being snatched out of the transport vehicle and escorted to the Restrictive Housing Unit (RHU), i was verbally and physically assaulted. They shouted racial epithets of, in this context, "boy," said "You must not know where you're at," called me "nigger," etc. At the same time, the chain linking the shackles together were repeatedly stomped on, causing shackle burns on my naked skin, breaking the skin, and, in fact, causing deep gouges into my ankles and Achilles tendon, leaving the area to look like raw bloody meat. Picture the image of a runaway slave who has run for miles in shackles.

i was then taken into a corridor with approximately seven guards who had their faces covered with scarf-type masks with patriotic symbols on them, and i was beaten while handcuffed in trip gear that included a black box, waist chain, shackles, and more. i was kicked, punched, and kneed, causing gouges in my head, a separated left shoulder, damaged acromioclavicular joint, and other injuries.

The Cover Up

What i discovered is that this isn't an unusual occurrence or anything out of the norm. i discovered that it is the norm and represents a culture that targets all prisoners in general but New Afrikan/Black prisoners in particular. In fact, i knew during the actual beating and perpetration of this hate crime that they had done this before. The signals given between the perpetrators, the body strikes and blows, where and how they were placed, the alert that "We have blood" when my head wound started to bleed, which immediately stopped the assault. Then they attempted to intimidate me into silence and denied me medical treatment.

Terrorizing and torturing prisoners with mental health issues is common, like Jabri Brown, whose toilet would be turned off for days and weeks; who sometimes wouldn't be fed or be provoked so that he could be extracted from his cell and beaten. Once he was told by Correctional Officer Brinegar, "I love beating your ass." The provoking and then punishing of those who react is also common, like "ghost-traying," or not feeding you, claiming that you refused to eat, spitting in and tampering with your food, and just blatantly violating your human rights—all with the wink and laughter of ranking officers and the administration.

An internal investigation was launched and i filed grievances where the response from the warden and the findings of the prison investigation stated that my allegations of being beaten were "indeterminate." How, within a high-tech prison with cameras everywhere, can allegations of a hate crime and assault be ruled to be "indeterminate?" It either happened or it didn't! Then it was pushed up to the main office, the Special Investigation Unit (SIU), where an official finding was supposed to be turned over to the director of the Virginia DOC, Harold Clarke, and to the attorney general's office. i was informed by investigators that "they" said: "You started to run your head into the wall and that you were frustrated and said you couldn't take this shit anymore." "You were acting suicidal."

You know, it's in Black folks' DNA where Our heads just attack billy clubs, Our necks press against knees, and Our heads intentionally slip into hanging nooses! If i was banging my head into walls, acting suicidal, or if i was trying to harm myself, what were the guards doing while escorting me, while holding onto me? Why wasn't i placed on suicide watch and into a camera observation cell? Why weren't my clothes taken and why wasn't i issued a "suicide prevention smock?" Why wasn't a mental health officer contacted?

So, either self-harm and suicide are promoted, encouraged, and allowed, or it never happened.

i was later told by one of the primary investigators that his findings had been turned over to the local district attorney's office. i've seen no evidence or anything in writing confirming this. In fact, this same investigator weeks later came to the prison and called my former cellmate out for an interview. The person, Demarcus Gravely, was allegedly asked during this interview that was supposedly recorded, if i ever stated to him that i was a Black Panther member or identified myself as a New Afrikan. What would my politics, Nationality, or National Identity have to do with being beaten while handcuffed and shackled?

Why We Need Prison Abolition, Not Prison Reforms

This is an attempt to discredit, character assassinate, and distract. No one has been held accountable and i'm still held on the crime scene, writing at the same facility where all kinds of attempts are made to either provoke me or neutralize my ability to be active.

This is why We push prison abolition. This is too much power without any real checks and balances. Any time you can beat, kill, maim, or destroy other human beings without fear of accountability—that is too much power.

In the mountains of Virginia, where a type of patriarchal white nationalism dominates, the cultural insensitivity and reactionary violence permeates these prisons in this southwestern region of the commonwealth. To not get involved, to not demand accountability, is to also say you do not mind when We return back to society as damaged individuals full of rage and anger and/or suffering from psychological trauma. It is to say you endorse the cycle of catch and release, either because you're a direct beneficiary of the PIC or, in spite of all your claims of morals and values, you have lost touch with your own sense of humanity and common decency of what is right and just!

T. Platt, in discussing proposals to reform prisons, notes they "are invariably formulated within the framework of corporate capitalism and are designed to shape new adjustments to existing political and economic conditions." He continues:

> . . . establishment reform proposals are formulated and practically designed to shape Afrikan peoples adjustments to existing and ongoing eurocentric political and economic conditions . . . to the conditions of White Supremacy . . . . . . [this reformism] has helped to create probation and parole, the juvenile court system, reformatories and halfway houses, the indeterminate sentence, adjustment and diagnostic centers, public defenders, youth services bureaus . . . which has served to strengthen the power of the state over the poor Third World communities and youth. As the American Friends Service Committee has observed, "the legacy of a century of reform effort is an increasingly repressive penal system and Our corrupt courts dispensing assembly line justice."[23]

It is a self-fulfilling prophecy when the power structure, government agencies, and their proxies go into poor communities, oppressed ghetto colonies, and so-called inner cities, and tear down affordable housing and housing projects, and close down schools and hospitals, while allowing the police and "law enforcement" to soften up the natives by terrorizing the youth and the block, making it "soft" for gentrification—euphemistically called redevelopment. This forces migration and refugees from these cities and areas to relocate to other areas, sometimes where civil wars of reactionary violence have been going on for generations, where people are forced to survive off of the underground economy or drug economy, and who are now fighting over markets and hostile takeovers. A ghetto colony hostile takeover of a "hood" or community where the market is lucrative for the latest drug used as an escape or coping mechanism.

These same elements are forced into consolidated schools as more weapons magically appear. And as that self-fulfilling prophecy comes to life, then come the talking heads and opportunistic politicians talking about the increase in violence, the need for tougher laws, the expansion of the PIC. Here is the government and its racist institutions seeking to capitalize off of, exploit, and save the day while feeding more ghetto human commodities into the PIC. It's a win-win all around for the state who tolerates the collateral damage of a baby or young child hit by a stray bullet here or there, while a mass shooting or wave of overdoses might sweep through . . . Yet these politicians in DC like Biden got the audacity to talk about "war crimes" and genocide in Ukraine. But it's not a war crime when you chokehold or taser Us to death, even while handcuffed? It's not a war crime when so-called correctional officers beat and stomp Us while calling Us "nigger" and "boy?"

Defund the police, stop these imperialist meddling wars, and stop sending billions to Ukraine to fight proxy wars against Russia.

New Afrikan Folks in amerika Need Reparations!

SECTION III:
THE PRISON INDUSTRIAL COMPLEX

THE STRUGGLE AGAINST ORGANIZED WHITE SUPREMACY IN INDIANA PRISONS

Introduction

The IDOC has a rich history of Ku Klux Klan and white suprem-acist activity, as well as organized violence.[24] It was only after New Afrikan prisoners in particular started organizing and engaging in militant strikes that some of these abuses were curtailed and/or pushed (outside of the media spotlight). A lot of these racists who were up-and-coming through the ranks during the '70s and '80s are now in leadership positions as either policy makers at the Central Office or on the boards of private prisons or companies like Aramark. Their backgrounds shrouded in secrecy, they act as consultants while giving rise to a whole new generation of neofascists from their ilk.

In the 1980s, a crooked investigator at the Indiana State Prison tried to put a hit on John "Balagoon" Cole by offering two white convicts (who were allies) a deal if they would throw white gas in his cell and burn him alive. They refused and, in turn, exposed the plot. Later, during court proceedings, after a hostage situation, Charles A. Penfold [the investigator] admitted under oath on the stand that he tried to do this and he wasn't fired, demoted, or charged with attempted murder! In fact, the bastard would eventually be promoted and moved to the Central Office.

When i first went to Pendleton Correctional Facility in 1985, after the initial slave rebellion of February 1 that year, the lock-up unit known as the dungeon, was racially segregated. Blacks and whites could not come out together for recreation. All movement to the recreation yards happened in handcuffs and shackles. After a late-night argument between myself and a young dumb wannabe white supremacist inmate, i witnessed the guards pass him a knife the next morning before recreation time. They tried to run Us outside together and remove his handcuffs first, but i had a handcuff key and came out of my cuffs first. i gave him a chance to surrender his weapon. He refused, and i allegedly commenced stabbing him nine times until they were able to drag his ass out, clearly and firmly sending a message to the "good ol' boy" network that i had no intentions on being a victim. There are many instances of this nature.

Jail Guards Part of Organized White Supremacist Gang

Wabash Valley Correctional Facility is infested with white nationalist correctional officers (COs) and they make no secret about it. Some of it is just cultural and racial ignorance, but some of it is rooted in ideology.

They also have a firmly entrenched "good ol' boy" network of male *and* female pigs that are either older or have been there a while and are steeped in the racist tradition of targeting New Afrikans. People like Major Russell, Lieutenant Nicholson, Basinger, Alan Finnan, etc., all of them dudes came up through the ranks together. This is why they were so mad when i allegedly stabbed [the white inmate] Sexton.[25] He had been there over twenty years, was entrenched in their little racist networks, and would sit out there in earshot of prisoners and tell stories to the younger COs about how they used to beat Us and throw Us down steps while handcuffed. Seriously.

Several times while i was being escorted, the guards would act like they were talking among themselves, but were actually talking to me indirectly, about how they wish this was the old Secure Housing Unit (SHU) so they could teach troublemakers a lesson. i always made it clear that if you ever beat me, it's going to be a homicide!

And here is one of the problems now. Back when i used to hustle, etc., i had a couple of female COs that, i'll just say, i was extremely close with. i used to run counter-intel operations. One used to be progressive and a sympathizer to Our struggle, so i used to get a lot of inside intelligence and even photos. i actually had emails and photos of the inside of their towers, of all their weaponry, etc. i can say it now because they busted some of the phones i had with them stored in my email folders.

The point i was getting to is this: You now have a whole new young crop working the SHU who are fascinated by these stories of brutalization. They are nostalgic for a time gone by. A lot of them are young, white, nationalistic, and veterans who have been over to Iraq and Afghanistan with that oppressive and authoritarian bullshit and are bringing it back home to visit upon Us. Brother Khalfani Malik Khaldun can tell you. After he was accused and convicted of killing that CO, they psychologically tortured that brother for over a decade. Dirty motherfuckers used to go on the recreation pads and get bugs, crickets, grasshoppers, water bugs, etc. to put in his food trays . . . The same shit they were doing to me on a smaller scale before i went on that hunger strike.[26]

You cannot claim to be radical, revolutionary, or anti-imperialist and allow the state to define and set the rules of engagement. Ain't no such thang as legal resistance. A movement without any teeth or the ability—or even the desire—to bite or bite back when bitten is a paper tiger. i refuse to be a part of such because what that tells me is i can be killed or sacrifice my life and those responsible would not be held accountable or brought to justice. It ain't about pushing masculinity or false masculinity/bravado. To me, sometimes that argument is used as a cop-out and an excuse to not take responsibility. i don't advocate any type of reckless reactionary adventurism, but as a political line reflective of an ideology, it must be understood that the groundwork and foundation has to be established to develop the iron-binding capacity to hold neofascist terrorists accountable.

When i first came into the system in the '80s and got sent to Pendleton, right after the rebellion that Balagoon and Christopher "Naeem" Trotter allegedly initiated, it was common for pigs to wear Klan rings, for them to call you "boy," or catch you isolated and call you "nigger."[27] At the State Farm in Putnamville, they were extremely vicious: chaining brothers to tables and shit, and beating them.[28] The stress positions and other torture techniques that they showed u.s. troops doing at Abu Ghraib was nothing new to us. Some of us were going through that shit at eighteen, nineteen, twenty-years-old.

The Need for a Mass-Based Movement Outside the Bars

It wasn't left-facing 'til dudes started organizing, taking over shit, and demanding that the feds come in . . . it wasn't until then that We started serving notice on racist pigs that justice was a double-edged sword, that We were able to push back some of the more blatant viciousness. Yet, that came at a price. Balagoon did thirty-five years in the hole. He and Naeem picked up another eighty to one hundred years. i've done over twenty-five years in the hole altogether. Had We had a strong, outside, mass-based political movement with an iron-binding capacity, then some of these comrades would not have had to make the sacrifices they did. Understand what i'm saying?

For some of Us, it's too late to try and retreat. i mean, i'm a lot older and more disciplined now. i'm not so quick to just jump out there without seeing the larger picture and what's at stake. With that being said, by the same token, the state ain't going to allow you to retreat; it's like the scarlet letter. And yet you can only kill me once.

The state murdered Ajamu Nassor (slave name Gregory Resonover) on December 8, 1994. They tortured him, electrocuting him until his head exploded in flames. While they were carrying out this act, they were playing **XXX HARDCORE FUCKIN' PORN TAPES ON THE PRISON CHANNEL ALL NIGHT!!!** Then the fascists threw a party in the administration building after the legal lynching was over. This was the epitome of disrespect and was extremely hurtful and traumatizing. Ajamu and Ziyon were Prisoners of War (POWs), codefendants, and highly respected and loved.

Approximately two weeks later, they found a neocolonial pig butchered in D cell house, a killing Khal [Khalfani Malik Khaldun] was later charged with. Once it got exposed how they tortured Ajamu, the fallout forced the state to stop using the electric chair and resort to lethal injection.

In the spring of 1996, it came time for them to murder his code-fendant, Ziyon Israel (slave name Tommie Smith), making him the first to executed in Indiana by lethal injection. This time, though, political forces had been quietly doing mass work and educating the population as to the politics and contradictions of the genocide penalty. By the time his date came around, large sectors of the prison were organized and mobilized. Various cell houses were carrying out nonviolent mass protests, with hundreds of prisoners in coordination with actions on the streets.

Because of what happened after they murdered Ajamu, and although the two events were never proven to be linked, the state moved to temporarily stay Ziyon's scheduled murder. Meanwhile, they manufactured all kinds of crazy conspiracy charges of planning to riot, to take over the prison, etc., and went to federal court to get an emergency order to move Us to a Maximum Control Complex (MCC). They moved twelve of Us for thirty days while rounding up tens of others at Indiana State Prison under the guise of an investigation. This was all after a silent protest in the kitchen of over two hundred prisoners of all nationalities. They panicked, made up a bunch of b.s. charges, and railroaded six out of the twelve of Us and shipped Us all across the state. Akono and i were sent back to MCC.

Before We were all moved, Ziyon was murdered on July 6, 1996. Tortured like Ajamu, he was poked with needles all over his body for over forty-five minutes. The state claimed they couldn't find a vein. During the course of the murder, there was militant action on all of the lock-up units. Mass flooding occurred in the administration building. Cells were destroyed by snatching the toilets and sinks out the walls, and Balagoon and them allegedly engaged in hand-to-hand combat with the goon squad as they went from cell to cell doing extractions. The twelve were immediately shipped, but the protest continued and a CO named Patikis ended up being stabbed through the bars by a young comrade as they refused to lock down and engaged the goon squad.

This is why i haven't been allowed to return back to Indiana State Prison since 1996. Everyone has since been allowed back over the years, except for me.

These were different times, and a different era altogether. However, it was also a product of the mass work that was taking place on both sides of the wall.[29]

CHAPTER 12

REAWAKENING A SLEEPING GIANT

In the 1970s, 1980s, and throughout the 1990s, there was a strong progressive, revolutionary prison movement throughout the state of Indiana. The two dominant and often competing political lines or ideologies were Revolutionary Nationalism, or New Afrikan Communism, as represented by the NAIM, and Afrikan Internationalism, as represented by the Afrikan People's Socialist Party. Other tendencies were represented by anarchists, Marxists, and Maoists.

During this time, you not only had loose networks of structure; you had a climate dominated by political or cultural consciousness. You also had hard-fought-for and hard-won institutions in prisons, such as ethnic studies, including the Black History class taught by prisoners. You had The Lifers' Organization that was run and operated by prisoners.

In fact, prisoners, or convicts, and prison clerks ran a parallel shadow system to the prison administration that actually made the prison functional and operational. If you wanted a bed moved or something done, you didn't go to a counselor; you went to an inmate clerk.

It was also common to see prisoners, some of whom were street organization-affiliated, holding political education classes out on the yard. In fact, it was mandatory for certain sets that you attend and go to school if you didn't have a General Education Diploma. At Pendleton Correctional Facility, for example, there was a program called the "Unity Run," where brothers of different affiliations got together out on the recreation yard in military formation—two abreast—and ran laps around the yard and did other exercise routines.

Around 1991, the IDOC launched a COINTELPRO-style counterinsurgency behind the walls. A concept and strategy known as the "Shock Doctrine" was a part of this counterinsurgency.

Hence, We saw the opening of Indiana's first Super-Maximum Security Prison, then known as the MCC, where some of the most vicious, repressive, violent, and psychological torture tactics were being deployed against its captives, the majority of whom were either PPs, conscious individuals, or prison rebels that the state wanted to break or make examples out of. It was used as the modern-day slave-breaking plantation, just like Abu Ghraib.

Most of the New Afrikan political leadership was held in this unit and then, later, the newly built SHU at Wabash Correctional Facility when it opened several years later. All organized political expression was under attack and being crushed by the Shock Doctrine application of outlawing prisoner groupings—primarily among New Afrikans. Controlled movement was implemented by installing fences and gates that confined Us into small areas and chopping off the heads—removing and isolating all threatening political leadership that wasn't going along with the program.

They also exploited and capitalized off of internal contradictions, petty differences, and jealousies within the ranks. Some residues of that still exist today, some twenty-five years on. While isolating conscious prisoners, they intentionally allowed the more reactionary elements of the population, such as street organizations (so-called gangs) and groups that were pushing racist ideologies, to flourish and establish operational bases. Utilizing this tactic, they shipped out many of the old heads, veterans, and OGs who had been down for fifteen to twenty-plus years.

Their security levels were lowered and they were moved to lesser-security prisons. Meanwhile, the younger prisoners coming in with significant time—often affiliated and unaware of the history of struggles and sacrifices—were sent to the maximum-security prisons. As a result, We have what We have today.

However, with the rise of the NALC and a few other lesser-known, more clandestine formations, there is a new current blowing throughout the state—countermeasures to the state's counterinsurgency. Let Our politics function like a contagious disease that spreads and infects the system's most vital organs until We cause it to go into cardiac arrest!

The New Afrikan Liberation Collective and Other Clandestine Groups Threaten the State

Today's prison slavery and privatization are incurable due to the big money private prison companies, like GEO Group, donate to political campaigns. For example, consider the $2 million GEO donated to former Governor Mike Pence or the $10,000 they gave to local congressmen to build the New Castle Correctional Facility in his district.

GEO attempted to do the same in Gary, Indiana, by offering to build a new immigration detention facility. The people organized against it and successfully blocked the plan. The fact that they would target Gary, Indiana—one of the most economically depressed and neocolonized cities in the state—and try to build an immigration detention facility there, try and hire poor, oppressed New Afrikans to watch over and control other poor, exploited, and oppressed people of color, demonstrates exactly how the system divides and conquers.

This is just another example of how the state and the system of capitalism manipulate and push the poor, oppressed, and disenfranchised communities aside or up against one another. Now, they manipulate poor New Afrikans, Latinos, and poor euro-amerikans to fight over crumbs and scraps from the ruling elites' table. They have Us blaming and scapegoating each other—and other exploited communities—to the point that We fail to critique or critically analyze this capitalist system as a whole, a system that keeps its foot on Our collective neck.

Some may rest on privilege—believe that they're a step above the rest—because they're standing *by* the stove and not sitting *on* the flame (like some communities are). i believe that is a false sense of both security and superiority. You're still getting heat, and capitalism, when it suits its purpose, will throw your ass directly into the fire. i predict that the Trump administration, in the end, is going to prove this analysis correct.

The same principle applies to prison politics of the struggle. Some sectors of the prison population allow themselves to be used and manipulated for certain privileges, like securing the best jobs, skilled jobs, strategic positions. These groups often turn a blind eye while the state attacks prisoners of color or represses religious groups, such as the Moors, Muslims, or the Hebrew Israelites.

Again, they don't understand that the state uses such disunity to manipulate Us all while preparing to repress and oppress Us all.

With that being said, as part of this strategy, We see the state moving to institutionalize a "class structure" among prisoners in Indiana while hardening the physical structure of maximum and medium-security facilities. They are adding more gates, fences, cameras, sophisticated surveillance technology, and catwalks on top of their prison walls. Simultaneously, they prepare to turn its older maximum-security prisons, like Indiana State Prison and Indiana State Reformatory, into primarily lockdown facilities.

By turning all cell houses into lockdown units, they are adding over two hundred beds to administrative segregation. Dorms and smaller housing units are being converted into honor housing. They are implementing Plus Programs, ACT Programs, and other behavior modification courses designed to supply the workforce to operate the prisons. Refuse to work? You're sent to an administrative segregation idle unit, where visits are limited to video or tablet-only contact, and phone calls are reduced to fifteen to twenty minutes per week.

You can already see the blueprint for this. Some housing units—where extra visits, food orders, video games, and commissary orders are allowed as a privilege—are being used to force prisoners to police one another's behavior and conduct. If you live in a dorm and a person gets caught with a knife, or a batch of wine, the entire dorm's extra privileges are taken, restricted!

There's a science to it. It makes you believe that, based on these privileges, you're not only different, but better than other prisoners. It becomes Us—the *"privileged" prisoner class*—vs. *them*—over there! These divisions are the winds blowing through the state of Indiana's prisons.

Recently, the state has, quickly and without media attention, implemented a program of disappearing prisoners who dare to fight back against the physical aggression from prisoncrats. These prisoners are being sent out of state without notification, due process, or appeal rights. This happened to Comrade Brother Cortez Wheeler, who was charged back in November 2017, alongside Brother Kimo, with three counts of battery with serious injury against prison guards.

The situation evolved after COs disappeared and withheld personal mail. As soon as Cortez signed a plea, he was shipped out of state and disappeared; supposedly, this is the IDOC's new response to all alleged serious assaults on prison staff. The state is so vindictive that they even refused to list his location on the IDOC locator website where friends, family, and supporters could reach him. It simply says, "out of state."

This should be an indication of what's to come. Today, those who allegedly injure COs are being shipped out of state. Tomorrow, it could be you. PPs with histories of struggle behind these walls and in these dungeons are already being threatened!

This is why the NALC, Prison Lives Matter (PLM), and IDOC Watch are so critically important right now. For one, it is to serve notice that We are here and aren't going anywhere. It also signals to the state and its prisoncrats that their policies and oppressive tactics currently in the dark shall be brought to light, and not only will they be exposed, but they will be held accountable. We want to hold these prisoncrats and politicians accountable for the people and the public.

Public Education by Revolutionary Prison Groups is Critical

We want to educate the public on the negative impact new sentencing guidelines have had on families, communities, and the prison population itself. These guidelines are being used as part of a larger scheme to build and expand county jail facilities throughout the state, particularly in areas where there are now complaints about overcrowding or a lack of resources.

We want the public to know that the IDOC implemented a policy in 2015 denying Us the right to apply for the restoration of good time, which has (often illegally) been taken from for those found guilty. As a part of this scheme, in February 2017, the IDOC commissioner issued a new executive directive ruling that, for certain serious assaults on staff or other offenses, *all of your credit time can be taken—and you can never get it back*!

If you've served twenty years, they can take all twenty years, thereby extending your release date and statutory sentence of the underlying felony by however many years they arbitrarily decide to take: no criteria, no guidelines, no checks or balances in place. Such practices violate the ex post facto clause of the constitution.

What these measures do is not only turn every incident into a potential life sentence; they also provide job security for these social parasites. They keep contracts, like the IDOC–GEO Group contract requiring the maintenance of 95 percent-plus bed capacity at the New Castle Correctional Facility, compliant.

We want to expose the Ferguson-style system of false reporting, where false tickets and write-ups are issued with little to no evidence. We are, then, sent before these disciplinary kangaroo courts for hearings, where often the chairperson or hearing officer is related to the captain, lieutenant, or supervisor—sometimes even by marriage—who signed off on the ticket. These blatant conflicts of interest are ignored and rubber stamped through a sham appeal process by the warden's office.

People need to be educated on, exposed, and enlightened to these hidden facts. Our families and communities need to see why We aren't coming home on time, why some of Us are getting more time, why We're being denied contact visits with Our families for five to ten years, or why We're being held in administrative segregation or solitary confinement for five to ten years or more.

Several guards at Pendleton Correctional Facility were recently fired for beating on handcuffed prisoners, as they did to Comrade Kwame Shakur—a story reported in the *San Francisco Bay View*.[30] Here We had the warden all over the news, lying about what "would not be tolerated." Yeah, especially when it's caught on camera!

Those of Us who are or have been housed at that prison know that the same sergeant has been beating and assaulting handcuffed prisoners for years, with full knowledge by a wink-wink approval from the administration. In fact, he was one of the administration's attack dogs and shakedown artists, often planting evidence and weapons on prisoners.

These are serious and dangerous times in this country. We can no longer afford to allow the state to dominate and dictate the narrative and control the information going out to the public about what's happening behind the iron curtains of these concentration camps. This is why it is so important for Us to support media—publications like the *San Francisco Bay View*—who try to hold it down for Us. Most of Us can come up with $24 in funds or stamps for a subscription.

We must signal to prisoners that while We must hold the IDOC accountable, We don't have to totally depend on the state. We can and must take some responsibility for Ourselves.

They don't want to fund or allow Us programs? Then build and organize your own! Create your own library, which should be mandatory for all NALC cadres.

That $50 or $60 you're spending on hood novels, sports magazines, or booty pics can be used to invest in some law books. Order medical encyclopedias or dictionaries where you can look up the medication they're giving you and learn about their side effects. Learn how to diagnose yourself and one another so that when you file a complaint or lawsuit about medical malpractice, you know what you're talking about.

Recently, the new health-care provider that replaced Corizon has instructed its doctors to discontinue prescribing and distributing all pain medications and to substitute them with psychotropic medications. A lot of these pills cause impotence, sterility, and kidney and liver damage. Look it up. A lot of the medications that are being used to treat mental health issues, like Zoloft, Cymbalta, etc., also have severe side effects. This is no coincidence—it's a concerted effort to saturate the population with psychotropic medications.

Doped up on bullshit, you lose interest in your rights or in resisting. You just want to sleep or mentally escape.

We often complain that We have no outside support. We will always have the naysayers and negative, toxic people that complain and critique but never initiate anything.

Yet there are people and organizations willing to help Us, support Us, and be Our voice. They are committed and not caught up in your affiliation, what city you're from, or your so-called race. They are organizing networks of lawyers to look into civil and human rights violations. They are people who are building media outlets to share information, who are lobbying Human Rights Watch and Amnesty International to investigate IDOC practices. They are educating, recruiting, and organizing in various communities and on college campuses about laws, Our prisons, and Our conditions. They are people who are in various communities and on college campuses educating about, recruiting, and organizing against these prisons, laws, and conditions.

Prison Lives Matter: A Strategy for Liberation

We're pushing Prison Lives Matter as part of a larger strategy towards liberation. Surely, if these organizations can represent Us and be in solidarity with Us, We can reciprocate. If We don't, who will?

We're pushing *Prison Lives Matter* to build, develop and unify political cadres capable of impacting other cells and atoms as they circulate throughout the bloodstream of the system.[31]

A reawakening of political consciousness. A stirring of "We're tired of this shit!" A developing critique of how We are treated, how the IDOC is out of control, and how it functions as a law unto itself. This developing climate—this gust of fresh air—is what i now speak to; it is to that reawakening.

These are strong winds blowing. Don't wait until the middle of a hurricane to try and build a structure or seek shelter from the debris and lightning. By then, it's too late, and you're likely to be overwhelmed.

Free All Political Prisoners!

CHAPTER 13

THE MANY FACES OF MENTAL HEALTH BEHIND THE WIRE

Within the context of a prison, i.e. penal facility, mental health both manifests and displays itself in many forms.

A lot of Us who enter into the PIC come from the lower socio-economic strata of society and arrive with some form of existing psychosocial issues, whether they hide or conceal themselves behind experiences with various kinds of abuse, from substance abuse disorder to sexual assault.

Mental health issues and "conduct" are now being criminalized and placed into that context. The state and its agents respond to someone with mental health issues as if they were a criminal. This triggers the full weight of the oppressive and repressive state. This also triggers more physical abuse, solitary confinement, verbal abuse, beatings, manhandling, disrespect, and disregard by a people who are often untrained, overworked, underpaid, and ill-equipped to deal with mental illnesses.

So, someone who hears voices, is delusional, who might have PTSD, anger, or rage issues, doesn't take care of their hygiene, suffers paranoia, and so on, becomes a "disciplinary problem" to be further controlled and repressed; they are hidden away in segregation units, isolation units, placed into camera cells on suicide watch while stripped naked and clothed in suicide prevention smocks, only to have their good time taken away from them and their sentences extended. All the while, another layer of job security employees of the state repressive apparatus.

Then, these same employees become resentful, hateful, and vindictive due to working in an already high-stress environment they didn't sign up for. i've seen prison guards and prisoncrats commit some of the most vicious, abusive acts against those who truly needed proper medication or mental health treatment, only to later laugh and joke about it.

The flip side of this is that those of Us who enter the system after suffering from issues that We have never been diagnosed for, or those of Us who have grown up in communities or environments that are war zones, or where civil wars are raging over so-called "beefs," territory, and/or markets connected to the underground economy, where We have witnessed or seen a body before the age of thirteen, have lost childhood friends to violence, and have lost a parent (or parents) to the drug game or the PIC.

It has always angered me to hear government officials and other agencies talk about military veterans coming back from foreign wars who have PTSD and/or other mental health issues due to their experiences, while We have children in Our communities witnessing school shootings and street souljahs who have been involved in shooting wars, children and family members who have been buried or who have bodies under their belts. Ain't no Red Cross for Us, ain't no Veteran Affairs or benefits for Us, ain't no military courts for Us where convictions and felonies get deferred or mediated. Instead, the only things left for Us are life sentences, extended aggravated sentences, and a slow death.

The same applies to those of Us who have fallen victim to the government campaigns of chemical warfare that are raging in Our communities. Don't talk to Us about alleged weapons of mass destruction hidden in the Middle East when Our communities are saturated with meth, crack, heroin, and every illicit drug known to man.

While We grow up in order to escape a deplorable and harsh reality, We often have to find ways to cope or escape, only to end up in the PIC. There, the side effects or aftereffects of years of drug abuse often go misdiagnosed or undiagnosed altogether. There, they are looked upon as disciplinary issues, when in fact some of these children have been traumatized in the ghetto colonies of amerika; they have been smoking embalming fluids and experimenting with all kinds of chemical cocktails; they have suffered all kinds of mental health issues that go untreated.

If We aren't cutting Ourselves (some do), or threatening suicide (some do), We don't receive treatment. If We're fortunate enough to get into a program, many of them are racially and culturally biased, and not grounded or rooted in a reality that many of Us come from or plan to return back to.

Many of these programs, including reentry programs, fail to adequately prepare Us to return back to society and avoid being reincarcerated. In some instances, in fact, they are just another way to get federal funding for programs that have no real substance.

Once again, many of Us are shoved through the cracks of the system, only to get trapped in the vicious cycle of catch, release, and return; caught in the cycle of carrying these mental health issues into Our communities, only to exacerbate already existing social ills and issues. A never-ending cycle of genocide!!!

FREE THE LAND!!

CHAPTER 14

DOMESTIC EXILE: LOW-INTENSITY WARFARE

Hidden from public view and without any real political or judicial oversight, the PIC has been forcing revolutionary PPs, prison rebels, jailhouse lawyers, litigators, and others into domestic exile.[32] Historically, and as a matter of routine, the Federal Bureau of Prisons has always moved its federal prisoners around the country, out of the state where they were convicted, as a matter of course.

This tactic has since trickled down to the state level. Now, various state DOC, as a part of a larger strategy of psychological warfare, ship prisoners out of state, thousands of miles away from Our families and support networks. This is no coincidence and, in fact, is being orchestrated and coordinated on a national level.

COINTELPRO and Counterinsurgency Behind the Walls

During the height of the Civil Rights Movement and what's known as the Black Power Movement, the federal government—through its various security and intelligence agencies, spearheaded by the FBI—initiated a counterinsurgency and counter-revolutionary program known by the acronym COINTELPRO (Counterintelligence Program):

> On July 15, 1969, Hoover publicly announced that all of the black nationalist groups, "the Black Panther Party, without question, represents the greatest threat to the internal security of the country." . . . by the fall of 1968, the FBI was secretly developing what would become its

> most intensive program to repress any black political orga-
> nizations. Of 295 actions initiated by the FBI's Coun-
> terintelligence Program to destabilize black nationalist
> organizations, 233 of them—or 79 percent—targeted the
> Black Panther Party. Federal actions against the Panthers
> ranged from spreading false information about misap-
> propriation of party money to fomenting initial strife,
> and, in some cases, participating in planned killings of
> Panther leaders . . . COINTELPRO aimed to undermine
> the Black Panthers ability to threaten the political status
> quo. Toward that end, its agents tried to foster divisions
> between the Panthers and potential recruits and between
> the Party and other organizations, as well as among the
> Black Panthers themselves.[33]

This program systematically targeted any political, militant, or
revolutionary organization that threatened the political status quo.
As pointed out above, the Black Panther Party (BPP) and later the
Black Liberation Army (BLA) were its primary and most principal
targets for destruction. As stated by the war criminal J. Edgar Hoover,
the BPP represented the biggest internal security threat to the u.s.
government and power structure that ever existed.

What a lot of people have failed to recognize—and what remains
crucial to understand—is that as state security forces targeted Our
political and militant organizations on the streets, murdering or
"neutralizing" Our leadership and cadre, they were simultaneously
carrying out a systematic program behind the walls. Many of the
newer generations and younger, up-and-coming revolutionaries have
failed to make this connection, even as they continue to be targeted
and victimized by this same government program.

As the Panthers, BLA cadre, and others were being hunted, murdered, framed, or forced into exile on the streets, We saw the assassination of Comrade George Jackson. We saw the brutal, murderous
repression of the Attica Rebellion. We also saw the murder, isolation,
and disappearing of countless of other brothers and sisters who
were part of the movement that were behind the walls. The state
declared and waged war on revolutionary brothers and sisters who
were trapped behind enemy lines. The same COINTELPRO tactics

that were being used against Us on the streets also came behind the walls. This is how Ruchell "Cinque" Magee or Hugo Pinnell (RIP) could do three decades in solitary confinement.[34] This is how the Angola Three, Herman Ferguson, and many others can be buried alive in isolation for over thirty years.

Now fast forward to the 1980s. You see, the state is a master at deception. With one hand they giveth and with the other hand they murder and taketh away. A lot of hard-fought human and prisoner rights were won in the 1960s and 1970s, when the Supreme Court and other circuit courts were forced by the activism and sacrifices of prisoners and Our allies, comrades, and supporters to give certain concessions on issues of due process, religious rights etc. It was also a tumultuous time in the country as far as various movements, resistance, and struggles for political power, reforms, human rights, and National Liberation. The state learned from their mistakes and losses during this time. They learned from the prison movement as it was spearheaded by Comrade George and Muslims, many of whom belonged to the Nation of Islam during that period.

Supermax Prisons: A New Scientific Approach to Counterinsurgency

So, moving into the 1980s, in an attempt to avoid a repeat of that era, the state moved towards the building of Control Unit Prisons and Super-Maximum Security Prisons with the opening of the Lexington Control Unit and with the replacement of Alcatraz Federal Penitentiary with the Marion Control Unit in Marion, Illinois. While prisons have always had dungeons ("holes") where they attempted to crush any form of resistance, this new development represented a more scientific approach. Instead of outright brutal murder and torture, the state improved the use of various behavioral sciences and moved towards a more methodical approach of total social isolation and sensory deprivation.

They created and used of all sorts of scientific behavioral modification programs, programs designed to break you mentally, physically, and spiritually. A new slave-breaking program of destroying your personality and rebuilding you in the image of the state. They continued perfecting the act of divide and conquer, creating class divisions amongst the ranks of prisoners, i.e. those who went along with or participated in the behavioral modification programs (now euphemistically called "step down rrograms" or "transition programs"), and the like. These programs now geared towards that of cell-bossism, self-policing, and the policing of other prisoners for class privileges.

In the 1990s, the rise of supermax prisons would catch on and spread like wildfire. As lawsuits were filed about various Constitutional and human rights abuses, as political movements, groups, and formations arose to fight this new trend of state repression and some units were exposed for human rights abuses and slated for shutdowns, the state shifted gears again. A lot of this resistance on the outside was spearheaded by the awesome work of the Committee to End the Marion Lockdown (CEML) and their newsletters *Cages of Steel* and *Cold Storage*.[35] The exceptional work by dedicated lawyers from the People's Law Office also had a significant impact, particularly out here in the Midwest. The state attempted to adapt and continued to evolve its barbarism with the rise of Pelican Bay, the ADX in Florence, Colorado, the SHU in Carlisle, Indiana, or the Maximum Control Complex (MCC) in Westville, Indiana. MCC being the first state supermax ever condemned by an international human rights organization for its human rights abuses.[36]

These units were used to target PPs and POWs and they were used to target the political leadership of both existing and up-and-coming political formations. They were also used as tools of intimidation as the state pushed a form of bogey man politics in an attempt to repress jailhouse lawyers/litigators, prison rebels, influential prisoners, and future revolutionaries.

The enemy state was using a multi-prong attack of:

1) Targeting leadership and PPs/POW for future repression and isolation; and

2) Trying to prevent the rise of a new prison resistance movement by attempting to kill it while it was still in its infancy still in the womb so to speak.[37]

While what's known as the prison movement and prison resistance in general have never been completely stomped out, you do have what's known as the ebb and flow of the movement, or a movement with both a low tide and a high tide.

As i wrote earlier, the enemy state brought the "Shock Doctrine" behind the walls. They started putting up fences, dog kennels, and gates everywhere, blocking Us off into small sections. They began hardening the facilities even more with new sophisticated surveillance and monitoring technology. They implemented control movement and tightened up internal security, all the while reducing and removing institutional programs and jobs.

They stopped building the old-school model prisons with four or five tiers stacked on one another and started building these prefabricated prison pods put together like Rubik's cubes, where various-sized groups could be watched more closely, where prisoners could be psychologically profiled, classified, and moved around or manipulated on the pod chessboard. Just as police security forces on the streets are being militarized—formed into tactical units with the latest military toys put to civilian use—the same is being applied to prison Special Emergency Response Teams (SERT) and Special Operation Response Teams (SORT). In fact, a lot of military veterans from u.s. imperialist wars are returning back to the u.s. and these kinds of police, security, and correctional agencies where military tactics, counterinsurgency, urban warfare, and torture/repressive tactics against "terrorists" are taught and adopted.

Renovating a Return to Repression: The State Absorbs Critiques

With the release of the book *The New Jim Crow* by Michelle Alexander, all of the liberal left and liberal elite wanted to jump on the bandwagon of critiquing the criminal (in)justice system—critiquing everything but neocolonialism.[38] But i digress. With this critique came the blatant exposure in disparities of sentencing and the institutionalized racism and genocide built into the system itself—realities and contradictions that oppressed nations and peoples have always been aware of.

In this critique, it was exposed that long-term solitary confinement causes mental deterioration, PTSD, and constitutes a form of psychological torture. As i mentioned in Chapter Ten, it constitutes a violation of the UN's "Mandela Laws." It also revealed that states with crumbling schools and infrastructure and other social ills could no longer justify or rationalize spending millions of billions of dollars on the so-called criminal justice system.

There had to be a public shift—or at least the perception of a shift—in the conversation on prisons and mass incarceration. As usual, the neofascist enemy state employed the art of smoke and mirrors, engaging in subterfuge. Instead of true or real reforms the capitalist state is incapable of doing, they attempted to apply a band-aid to a major trauma wound. Instead of major surgery, we get cut, paste, and stitch. For example, now that it has become fashionable and more cost-effective to take a look at long-term solitary confinement, the state is adding old tactics in new forms to its arsenal of repression and control.

This low-intensity warfare is manifesting in the opioid epidemic behind the walls and the rise of psychotropic medications as a cure-all for anything from a common headache to psychotic behavior. Just as the popular TV series "Snowfall" depicted the rise of the crack epidemic in California spearheaded by the CIA and federal government back in the '80s, so today terrorist and white supremacist pigs move poisonous synthetic forms of weed that have been treated with various chemicals like roach spray in Our prisons. Some shit that got these dudes falling into comas, violent seizures, or dropping dead altogether.

Then there are tactics like forcing Us to consume contaminated water while building prisons in cancer corridors on contaminated soil. Why are so many prisoners and PPs/POWs dying from cancer-related issues within a short amount of time of their release? They have served over twenty or twenty-five years in these death camps! Why are so many of Us developing kidney, liver, and heart diseases and other issues across the board—regardless of nationality and whether you are vegan, vegetarian, workout, or whatever? In this case the nationality is "convict."

Additionally, there is the state's manipulation of gang warfare and racial hostilities as part of low-intensity warfare. Using these reactionary forces, the state targets some PPs/POWs, especially the more active and vocal ones, including some of Our elder PPs who can't adequately physically defend themselves. This isn't a coincidence. This leads me to the main reason i wrote this piece. i want to address something that isn't being talked about, or at least not in the proper context, in my humble opinion. That is the practice of sending state prisoners into domestic exile by subjecting Us to what's officially called the Interstate Corrections Compact: an agreement between states where they will exchange, swap, or accept prisoners from other states, jurisdictions, or counties other than their own.

Sold off the Plantation

On December 18, 2018, in the wee hours of the morning i was packed up, chained up, and thrown in the back of a paddy-wagon-type van (equipped with an infrared camera) and sent on a fourteen-hour ride to the neoconfederate state of Virginia, without any form of due process. i was not allowed to pack my own property; a squad of fifteen police did that while i was held in the shower for over two hours with a sentry posted outside the door while other team members assembled a high-tech electronic pole that detects any form of metal to ensure that i did not have a phone, cuff key, or knife shoved up my rectum.

In fact, i wasn't even told where i was going during the drive. The windows were covered so i couldn't see out the windshield to read highway signs. i had to search license plates on cars on to determine what state i was in. In every state, We stopped for a fifteen-minute bathroom break and i was fed a dry peanut butter and jelly sandwich.

Prior to leaving the facility, i was given and forced to wear and travel with a pair of shower shoes, not my own or from my property. i would later discover that the shower shoes were contaminated with some kind of sour smelling fungus. Initially the smell was at a low to medium level like sour milk. After three weeks, i finally figured out it was the shoes. My cellie suggested We treat them with hot water and disinfectant until i could purchase a new pair. When We completed this process, the fungus exploded and actually contaminated anything it touched and, in fact, it permeated an entire twenty-tier area! The shoes had to be placed in two plastic bags and thrown away, along with clothes, socks etc. The cell had to be scrubbed. Had i continued to wear those shoes, who knows what damage would have been done to my feet and what poisons would have been absorbed into my bloodstream. Why were they substituted for my own personal pair in the first place? Diabolical!!

i discovered that this move had been orchestrated and signed off on by the governor, attorney general, and executive branch of the IDOC. i also discovered that i had been traded or sold for Comrade-Brotha Kevin "Rashid" Johnson, who had been moved to Pendleton Correctional Facility (PCF) in Indiana a couple of months earlier. PCF, as We saw earlier, has a long racist history of brutality and was the scene of the violent prison rebellion on February 1, 1985. The brotha has been in the state for approximately three months and still hasn't been given his personal property![39]

A New Fugitive Slave Act

In my research, i'm discovering that brothers and comrades who are either leadership, cadre, or who have continued to be active and rebuilding the movement, comrades whom the state has been unable to break—are being targeted all around the country for domestic exile, i.e. moving Us away from Our families and support networks solely based on Our ideological and political beliefs. The New Afrikan Black Panther Party – Prison Chapter's (NABPP–PC) cadre and leadership appear to be one of the principal targets thus far. Some comrades have been moved to three, four, or five different states within the last three years alone!

This method and strategy of the state is giving a whole new meaning to the Fugitive Slave Act! The higher courts have ruled that We have no reasonable expectation to be held or confined within Our state of conviction. Once again, this gives credence to the reality that We are being dehumanized as modern-day slaves, even as chattel. Once again, the Thirteenth Amendment statement, "Neither slavery nor involuntary servitude, except as a punishment for crime whereof the party shall have been duly convicted shall exist within the United States," is crystallized.

Doesn't this tactic violate Our so-called constitutional right of being free to believe and express Our religious and political beliefs without fear of retribution or retaliation from the state?? This is also psychological warfare that is being coordinated and orchestrated at some high levels of the state and its security agencies.

Removing Us from support structures of families, comrades, and supporters while disappearing Our legal materials, law books, family photos, etc. and subjecting Us to a foreign and potentially hostile terrain is meant to make you vulnerable, enhance your isolation, and—if possible—neutralize you by reactionary forces. When i was moved out here to Virginia, my television disappeared while in "storage," along with all of my law books that specifically focused on

Indiana state law and Seventh Circuit law—or those that contained evidence pertaining to a pending lawsuit—the Quran, Bible, and many other books. Law books that focused on federal law instead of Indiana law were all left untouched!

We are being moved without any form of due process, hearings, or heads-up, usually in a military fashion with heightened security. We are also being denied access to the courts. The law library here is mediocre, almost primitive, with no access to any Indiana codes, cases, etc.

Before the resignation of the reactionary former Attorney General Jeff Sessions, Oppressident Trump issued an order to Sessions to start a database classifying all prisoners who advocate "revolutionary Black nationalist politics, Black identity, or self-government ideologies" as domestic terrorists. While this is no surprise, this alone has serious and far-reaching implications in this era of hyper-anti-terrorist rhetoric. Some years ago, there was a discussion taking place in the federal government amongst prisoncrats about creating regional prisons for the so-called "worst of the worst." This means they're talking about taking the art of supermax facilities to a whole other level.

On the state level, before they started building supermax torture chambers, they were using the tactic of transit in an attempt to suppress and isolate PPs and revolutionary forces. This meant you were repeatedly being moved or shipped from one prison to the next. Every few months or at least once or twice a year, you were shipped to another prison in an attempt to keep you off balance and prevent you from building any type of type of foundation, political base, or social infrastructure. This practice was altered on the state level with the rise of the Control Unit and Supermax Prisons, where now the practice becomes isolation: they bury you alive for years on end.

Well, revolutionaries, PPs, and activists found a way to subvert that attempt at isolation. In fact, We flipped the script and turned a lot of these units and dungeons into schools/universities of revolutionary cadre development.[40] Turned them into base camps of resistance and struggle, e.g. George Jackson Universities, even more so with the advancement of various forms of technology. This isn't to say or suggest that some of Us aren't or weren't permanently damaged by this form of scientific torture or brutalization.

The Two Choices of Oppression

Repression breeds one of two things: either resistance or coward-
ice. You either find a way to fight back, to struggle forward, or you
surrender to the tyranny of the oppressor. Take the massive hunger
strikes and work stoppages throughout the penal colony of California
spearheaded by brothas slammed down in solitary at Pelican Bay. This
continued resistance and response by Our outside comrades and supporters has taken away some of the power of the state's tools that are
used to destroy and brutalize. This is occurring as We see under the
Trump administration with the u.s. withdrawal from UN Treaties
and Covenants on genocide, human rights protection of prisoners,
etc. In fact, the UN—with all of its hypocrisy and lack of democratic
practices—is now even more delegitimized.

As contradictions sharpen, as revolutionary formations continue
to rise behind enemy lines, the state must come up with some type of
Hitlerian "final solution." They must up the murder game and bring
it to Our leadership. Domestic exile based solely on Our politics and
practices allows the state sending Us to disavow having a hand in
nefarious attacks, while it allows the receiving state to disavow any
role in the orchestration of Our killings or assassinations. Isn't that
one of the key tactics of COINTELPRO, along with sowing seeds of
conflict and distrust? Why should it be any different for revolutionaries and movements behind the walls?

This is what We aren't discussing enough amongst Ourselves on
both sides of the wall. The narrative needs to be changed and put
into proper context. Ain't no such thing as legal revolution, legal
resistance. We all profess to know and overstand the nature of the
beast or enemy, and yet We don't prepare for or respond to their
murderous tactics.

When We expose their hidden agendas, this puts cover on and
security for targeted comrades because it serves notice that not only
are comrades' general welfare and health being monitored, but also
that Our enemies are being watched by outside forces and allies. It
serves notice that any suspicious attacks and/or murders of comrades
will not only be thoroughly investigated and exposed, but there must
and will be accountability on both sides of the wall.

National Infrastructure Building and Strengthening of Networks

The last few years have seen a rise in coordinated protests and resistance behind enemy lines, especially during the month of Black August. It is way past time for a revolutionary vanguard structure that represents and gives outside teeth to this resistance, teeth that can eventually bite. It's way past time that all of these various defense committees, small group support structures for PPs, etc. start not only talking together but building together, start to actually be absorbed into existing formations. The Jericho Movement has been putting in work for over twenty years. The material by comrades in FROLINAN and Jalil Muntaqim are even older and should be required reading![41] Recently, some of Us have begun to push for regional organizing committees comprised and representative of the most active PPs and POWs in that region and their support networks or structures. We want to eventually build some sort of national steering committee for the support of PPs and POWs and also for the resistance behind enemy lines, giving such resistance a point to the spear. This also helps to undermine the state strategy of forcible exile and isolation. When a comrade such as Rashid gets moved to Indiana or myself to Virginia etc., there's no reason why We shouldn't immediately and automatically be absorbed into and supported by those existing networks on both sides of the wall. In my case, NABPP–PC comrades not only made me feel welcome, but offered concrete assistance on both sides of the wall.

People, We have to get clear on a vision and Our political line. When you have a clear vision, a correct vision, it makes it easier to build. As We push for and build for revolutionary National liberation struggle, ultimately one of Our goals has to be to make these dungeons ungovernable. Shut this motherfucker down! Shut your profiteering down! No new prisons or Immigration and Customs Enforcement (ICE) facilities get built without the possibility of being sabotaged! The ultimate strategy can't be about reforms, making it a kinder, gentler oppression, or gaining UN recognition; it has to be about sharpening the contradictions of anti-imperialist struggle on both sides of the wall—where it becomes possible to call for mass protest, mass general strikes, accountability of known terrorist pigs. If We ain't envisioning that, if We ain't building towards that, or at least in that direction, then We playing!

At some point, We have to develop the capability to liberate comrades, PPs, and POWs that have been languishing behind enemy lines for thirty-five, forty-five plus years and now are in their '60s, '70s, and '80s. At some point, the qualitative leap has to be made from protest to active resistance. That has to be an essential element of that vision. A key part of facilitating that is the building of Revolutionary Organizing Committees and absorbing some of the Basic Units that already exist. Recently, some formations have put aside various petty differences, personal egos, and ideological differences and We have merged in an attempt to further strengthen and build those national networks i mentioned. This is also an effort to help strengthen networks of outside comrades and organizations as We move towards building that vanguard. Beyond just growling, We have to move in the direction of being able to bite!! This is Our time. All We have to do is seize it! East Coast, West Coast, Midwest, South—do y'all hear me?

In solidarity!
Re-Build!

CHAPTER 15

THE STRUGGLE FOR EDUCATION BEHIND THE WALLS

The average layperson who doesn't have any experience in dealing with the PIC would believe that prisons are all about rehabilitation and helping people come out as better human beings.[42] However, a lot of Us come out worse than when We went in, unless We took the initiative to do for Ourselves what the state would not do.

The PIC is about social control: controlling specific threat groups and populations or demographics that are a potential threat to the status quo and social order. The PIC is also about profiteering; this is why and how private companies like the GEO Group can profit over $1 billion annually. Prisons have never been about crime control and have always been about economics, exploitation, and slavery. Education in prison is used as a political prop and not to enhance or prepare Us for reentry into society. Education is used as a control mechanism. The state and various other institutions are quick to quote statistics of how many prisoners are enrolled and how many may actually graduate. They might even headline the local news channel. What isn't told is how many people who want to go to school in prison can't because of the waiting list or because of their sentence.

This isn't absolute or universal but is generally the rule.

What Isn't Told

What isn't being told is that, if i've caught a petty ticket, then i can't participate in a school program or i am removed from the one i'm taking. What isn't revealed are the obstacles placed in Our path if We try to take responsibility for Our own education or for one another's education.

On one hand, the state giveth, and with the other hand, the state takes away, by:

- Placing limits and restrictions on the amount of books We can have
- Counting law books and religious books the same as regular leisure or entertainment books
- Tightening up the policies and restrictions as to who can and can't send you books, where books can come from far as publishers, used books, Books Thru Bars programs, free books, etc.

The state is dramatically limiting Our access to education.

With the level of reactionary violence, prisoner-on-prisoner violence, you would think that in the interest of education, the PIC would want prisoners to have their faces in a book. Yet this is not the case at all. Why would or does the PIC feel threatened by prisoners who teach other prisoners, putting together study groups, or political education classes? These acts alone can get you shipped out to another prison, get your security level boosted, get you placed in solitary, or placed in the hole for gang activity—just because you're trying to learn from or educate others.

The State Knows Something Most Prisoners Don't

The state knows something that most prisoners don't: knowledge and education is self-empowerment and power. They are a threat to the profit motive and control of the state. Here is a stark reality that most people don't know. In most states, the DOC receives federal dollars and grants for having various programs on the books or operational in their facilities. This is no critique of the people who might teach prisoners and might even have Our best interests in mind, but they are just a cog in the overall machinery of the PIC. In most cases, if you do not have a short amount of time left to serve, then you can't even get into a program or class.

Here is how the business works. During your intake into prison and throughout your sentence, you're asked various questions and surveys as part of the classification process: Have you ever done meth or cocaine? Have you ever committed a sex offense? Have you ever thought about it? How often did you hit your wife or girlfriend?

Often, these probing questions are racially and stereotypically based and often culturally ignorant. But this stereotypical data is used to generate statistics so the DOC can release reports claiming 65 percent of incoming inmates have either used or been addicted to either meth or opiates, and they need x, y, z funds to create a program to treat such. This is job creation, people. This is part of the growth and continued development of the PIC.

It is this process that creates counselors, therapists, facilitators, and consultants, many of whom are either unqualified, disenchanted, or demoralized by a system that won't support them or give them the tools necessary to do their job. As a result, they just go through the motions and draw a paycheck. Sadly, a lot of the programs aren't reality-based in Our realities as Black or Brown men and womyn. These programs don't adequately prepare Us to return to a lot of Our communities. Many of Us are returning to areas that are economically depressed and oppressed, many have civil wars taking place underneath the surface around the drug economy and various markets related to such. Many of Us are coming out or have PTSD and other mental health-related issues of rage, anger, depression, or stress that go untreated. Talk therapy, counting to ten, and all of that ain't going to get it when you're in the "hood" after doing ten years or more, having spent x amount of time in solitary, and not being able to find a job that pays the bills.

Real Education Instills Hope and Faith

You see, when We have real education and treatment programs, they instill hope and faith. They give you other options, and they inspire creativity and thinking outside of the box. When you have agencies and community-controlled organizations active in the community around reentry and that are proactive in attacking the causes of recidivism and the rage visited upon Our community by so-called "ex-offenders" out of frustration, only then does higher education become both real and effective.

Be proactive now and you won't have to be reactive later.

Yours in Freedom & Justice.

SECTION IV:
CONTINUING THE STRUGGLE

CHAPTER 16

PALESTINE AND THE NEW AFRIKAN (BLACK) NATION

The colonization of a people, the theft of a people's land, and/or the theft of a people before imposing second-class citizenship upon them are crimes against humanity and International Laws that so-called Civilized Nations are supposed to be governed by.[43]

Similarities of Occupation and Domination

The colonization of a people, the theft of a people's land, and/or the theft of a people before imposing second-class citizenship upon them are crimes against humanity and International Laws that so-called civilized nations are supposed to be governed by. You have a government that—through political, economic, and/or military domination— oppresses, kills, and dictates the quality of life under the guise of being the chosen people, under the guise of zionism, under the guise of white supremacy, maintaining security, and a host of other bogus reasoning: that is an outlaw government, a terrorist state, a government that is guilty of genocide and committing crimes against humanity.

It's interesting how there are so many similarities between colonial oppression and occupation in Palestine and the ghetto colonies throughout amerika.

Both the united states and israel came to exist as settler-colonial powers predicated upon the genocide and erasing of Indigenous Peoples and communities, as well as the enslaving and slaughtering of Afrikan and New Afrikan People while occupying other people's land.

In occupied Palestine, land has been seized and redistributed. It is the same with New Afrikans and Indigenous folks, such as Native

Amerikans, and all throughout the South within the National Territory where Black folks worked, slaved, shed blood and tears, and engaged in war only to have their National Territory occupied, seized, confiscated, and redistributed, despite promises of forty acres and a mule. Only to be denied the right to Self-Determination, only to be denied the right to nationality while having one imposed upon you and amending you as a people into a constitution.

Just as in Palestine, you have soldiers and settlers policing the colonized, engaging in extrajudicial legal murders protected by the "law." You have the George Zimmermans, the cases of Sandra Bland, George Floyd, Brotha Aubrey, and too many others to name. You have instances where settlers and u.s. security forces have murdered unarmed civilians—same as in Palestine.

Throw a rock and get murdered, join a political or militant formation and challenge occupation and have your family evicted and your home blown up by a missile strike. In contrast, live in the projects, so-called affordable housing, and/or on reservation and get caught hustling to survive or challenging oppressive neocolonial power, and your family is evicted—grandma and everybody. Live in a high-rise project and be subjected to prison-style lockdown as cops (colonial occupational personnel) and tactical units and soldiers rush in with battering rams and carry out search-and-destroy operations!

Look at the Gaza Strip and West Bank during the protests and rebellions against colonial violence and you see tear gas, the firing of rubber bullets and live rounds, you see military vehicles and militarization. It kind of looks like Ferguson when Mike Brown was murdered, Minnesota when George Floyd was murdered, or Louisville when Breonna Taylor was murdered, or Watts, Compton, Crenshaw, Florence, or Normandie after the cops got off for beating Rodney King.

No, We don't have F-16s and gunships strafing Our communities like in occupied Palestine. We got ghetto birds doing twenty-four-hour surveillance and dropping improvised explosive device bombs on homes full of womyn and children. Example: MOVE Philly, May 13, 1985. Bombs dropped, murdering New Afrikan Revolutionaries and burning down an entire Black community. MOVE were called terrorists also!

No, We are not getting bombed by gunships, instead, We are getting saturated by chemical and biological warfare agents. We are victims of a racist ass Medical-Industrial-Complex that allows New Afrikan womyn to die in massive numbers during childbirth or from breast or ovarian cancer, and a ton of other illnesses, many of which are preventable or curable.

No, Our children and men (increasingly more and more womyn) are being ethnically cleansed from Our communities into the PIC.

These are just a few of the reasons that those of Us who represent the New Afrikan Independence Movement and the Black Liberation Movement stand in Solidarity with Palestine and all Neo-Colonized Peoples fighting against Genocide and Struggling to Free the Land!

Free The Land!!

CHAPTER 17

REVOLUTIONARY NOTES FROM THE WESTERN FRONT

Introduction

amerika has never dealt with its original sins of colonial genocide and structural settler racism; instead, it has moved to placate, to pacify, and co-opt New Afrikan/Black folks into its own structural system of oppression and neocolonialism.[44]

New Afrikan people represent an oppressed nation, an exploited nation—where the means of production and the ability to produce and sustain itself, the ability to meet the needs of its people and community—seized by a foreign entity. This genocidal seizure was to be in the interest of creating the amerikan settler state that later, on the surface, created this false impression of a multicultural democracy.

You don't get to impose a constitution upon a conquered people. You do not get to amend a people into a constitution that you once deemed as three-fifths human. You do not get to impose a second-class citizenship upon a people and call it "freedom," as if all has been forgiven and forgotten.

What is Freedom for New Afrikan People?

Freedom for New Afrikan people represents Independence, Land, Autonomy, and the ability to be Self-Determining in creating its own destiny and National Identity. It means being able to dictate and sustain the quality of life for Our people. It means being able to not only govern Ourselves but create institutions that meet the needs of

Our people, Our children, and have a direct impact upon Our material world, existence, and the quality of Our lives.

Freedom means being able to reverse some of the negative social ills impacting Our community in the areas of health care, economic empowerment, and economic independence, where We are no longer contributing trillions of dollars into an economy that is controlled by a government that has proven not to function in Our collective best interest, a government where We see very little of those trillions reinvested back into Our community or Our people, especially Our children or youth. Freedom means being able to put a stop to a lot of the reactionary and homicidal violence that exist in Our community. It means being able to stop and reverse the chemical and biological warfare being visited upon Our communities. It means ending and reversing the mass incarceration and current practice of harvesting and ethnic cleansing of Black and Brown bodies out of Our communities and processing them into the PIC.

We are Revolutionary Nationalists

We are not separatists; We are revolutionary nationalists, which is different and distinct from Black nationalism or reactionary nationalism. As an enslaved people once deemed chattel slaves by the u.s. government, as a conquered and neocolonized people based on international law, We were never allowed to declare Ourselves free and independent. We have never been allowed, through a legal entity or democratic process, to declare Our Nationality and National Identity and have it recognized and binding on this government. Nor have We been afforded reparations to make up and atone for the four-hundred-plus years of bondage, servitude, exploitation, and genocide perpetrated against New Afrikan people by this neofascist and neocolonial government.

Therefore, We continue to wage the struggle of war and resistance for Land, Independence, and Socialism first begun by Our ancestors when the first settlers stepped off the boats and arrived on the shores of Afrika. We salute, champion, and continue that tradition from one generation to the next.

As i tune into the corporate-controlled media and i see all of these young people and others who have suddenly discovered that genocide not only exists but is being perpetrated against the

Palestinian people by israel, i can't help but ask: do you not see the genocide that has been and is being carried out against New Afrikan/Black folks in modern-day Babylon?! Genocide that is being carried out on the shores of the north amerikan continent? We are pro-Palestine liberation as We are pro-Haitian, pro-Darfur, and pro-Sudan liberation. But We are also pro-New Afrikan Liberation. You do not have to look outside of the u.s. borders to denounce genocide. You have wars and struggles of National Liberation right here on this north amerikan continent: the thousands upon thousands of Native and Indigenous people being wiped off of this earth, the womyn being disappeared and slaughtered from their communities that no one wants to acknowledge or talk about, for example. The tens of thousands of Black and Brown bodies being fed into prisons that prevent Our ability to reproduce or serve Our people and Our communities.

Revolution Starts At Home!!!
We Challenge You To Broaden The Struggle!!!
Free All Political Prisoners!!!
Free The Land!!!

CHAPTER 18

SIGNPOSTS ON THE ROAD TO FREEDOM

The belief that prisons are about rehabilitation is a false narrative propagated by a billion-dollar industry that is becoming more lucrative everyday as the need for more and more social control of the "other" intensifies. This is occurring as so-called constitutional rights are rolled back and as government control and regulation invade more and more the province of Our private (colonized) lives. This is occurring as more and more socioeconomic mechanisms of control and monitoring are put into place to solidify the foundations and overarching authority of a police state.

The PIC and other institutions of so-called criminal justice cannot be separated from the history and legacy of this empire. This history is starkly represented in the fact that the u.s. incarcerates more of its so-called citizens than any other industrialized nation, and more Afrikan folk than anywhere else in the world.

We are dealing with systems of oppression and institutional power dynamics. It is not simply about individuals (e.g., good cop vs. bad cop) but about the power of oppressive institutions and their relationships to various oppressed or "disenfranchised communities." Those same institutions have a historical context and foundation that both liberals and revisionists try to either whitewash or deny altogether while stirring up "race" hysteria, attacking and scapegoating Critical Race Theory (CRT). This represents a modern-day version of the Crusades, of burning books and witches at the stake, as opposed to critiquing the very system itself and developing a radical analysis of how the very system gives rise to the social ills that impact Our lives.

For example, what does "disenfranchise" really mean? Where did it come from? Surely it didn't just appear but had to come from a power source—a deliberate policy and political practice enforced by the intentional marginalization and discrimination against specific groups and demographics. Smokescreens are used to hide and conceal the hidden hand of the real oppressive power and the social impact that power has on Our lives as individuals and as an oppressed, neo-colonized Nation of people. Some things are just so ingrained and unconscious that people don't self-critique or self-examine how they are affected by them. We don't critique space, power, privilege, and Our roles in facilitating oppression. Amos N. Wilson does:

> White supremacy, by its very nature and intent, requires the continuing oppression and subordination of Afrikan People; and in time, may require their very lives. Subordination of a people requires that the people in some way or ways be violated, dehumanized, humiliated and that some type of violence be perpetrated against them. The violently oppressed react violently to their oppression. When their reactionary violence, their retaliatory or defensive violence, cannot be effectively directed at their oppressors or effectively applied to their self- liberation, it then will be directed at and applied destructively to themselves. This is the essence of Black-on-Black Violence. Oppressive violence is both proactive and reactive, directed and mis-directed. Black men kill each other because they have not yet chosen to challenge and neutralize on every front the widespread power of white men to rule over their lives . . .

The constant increase in Black-on-Black violence and criminality reflects the constant incremental generation by prevailing socioeconomic conditions of Black hostility and anxiety fueled by a constantly increasing sense of futility. Thus Black-on-Black violence and criminality are danger signals, flashing red indicators of explosive social inequalities, dysfunctionalities, dislocations, and conflicts. They are alarming reminders that the White American-dominated body politic is diseased, in danger of cardiac arrest, and in need of radical surgery and intensive care.[45]

Thus, We see an increasing rise of, and a 2.0 version of, right-wing neofascism and extremism. Actually, We see two qualitative forms and a two-pronged attack: the above-ground and underground strategy for deepening fascism in amerika.

With the above-ground prong, there is the knee-jerk reactionary racism propelled into the mainstream stratosphere by Trumpism—a vicious and raw reactionism that helped to reveal the naked fascism at the core of amerika despite its liberal clothing. It was and is white nationalism in-your-face, up close, and personal. "Make amerika Great Again," "Take our Country Back, "Put dem Dirty Black and Brown Bodies and Terroristic Muslims Back in Their Place." That ideology and movement has now morphed into an attack on CRT. How dare you teach young white children about the history of this country or the crimes committed by their ancestors? How dare you deviate from the lies that have been taught and force-fed, as people pull down statues of mass murderers of Afrikan and Indigenous people?

As the progressive masses scream "no" and pull-down confederate statues and monuments to former slave owners, rapists, and baby killers, the ultra-right mobilizes its own ranks. A shockwave of consciousness and more "wokeness" has rippled through various segments of society like an electric current, and the science of dialectics dictate that there must be a reaction on the opposite side of that current. We see the rise of the ultra-right neofascism as it goes into a panic. We see how the ultra-right here in amerika is further strengthening and consolidating its neofascist ties with white supremacist groups in Europe.

There is the ultra-right panic provoked by young white kids joining up with People of Color, New Afrikan, and Latinx folk and screaming, "Black Lives Matter!" Screaming that they reject the vulgar consumerism that other generations have taught is the only thing that matters. There is a reactionary panic as today's younger generations engage in a genuine self-critique and reject their privilege, choosing not to participate or sanction the genocide and violence against Afrikan people, Indigenous people, and People of Color. New Afrikan children are discovering more and more their New Afrikan genius and taking pride in their natural beauty and glorious heritage. There is a reactionary panic as younger generations choose to reject the patriarchal b.s. they have been force-fed, choosing instead to self-identify and define for themselves who and what they are. This represents a threat to the status quo, to the establishment, and to the power base, that cannot be allowed. How dare you say the word "gay" or "trans"? These words are more dangerous to the reactionaries than the Resource Officers in Our schools beating and killing kids from poor communities, or than the predators sexualizing and sex trafficking Our children. How dare you be pro-choice and refuse to birth babies for the fatherland—for the capitalist labor pool?

With the other prong, the underground prong of the fascist offensive, you have the increasing rise of the right-wing paramilitary-political groups masquerading as patriots. You know, the Klan has undergone a Jerry Springer make-over. You know, "Papa Got A Brand New Bag!" They say the revolution will not be televised, but what about race wars—intentionally misidentified as cultural wars?

You know, the Proud Boys, the Oath Keepers, the Rise Above Movement, the 1 Percent, and the right-wing veterans that are coming back from foreign wars of slaughtering and "smart" bombing the "other," demoralized, angry, suffering from PTSD, defecated on by the very system to which they pledged allegiance and for which they lost comrades. They are now preparing to bring the war home, preparing to MaGA and flood the prisons as prison guards or "law enforcement," where all of their rage and violence is given free reign against those no-good, well-deserved, dehumanized, prison inmates—especially those who are political freedom fighters engaged in National Liberation Struggles and who share socialist ideologies—people in the spirit of Comrade George Jackson. Please do not let some of Us all be Muslims to you—where you now search Our cells and property, see books, literature, or Qurans that trigger your memory of homes, villages, and doors you kicked in during your raids and the materials you found. Please do not let Us all look Middle Eastern, Arab, or Asian Pacific, or in the likeness of the people you have been shooting, hunting, waterboarding, and bringing democracy to for the last twenty years!!

These ultra-right guards are the elements you saw storming the Capitol on January 6, 2022, in a coup attempt to reinstall Trump. These are the forces you see conspiring to kidnap and kill the Governor of Michigan and "found Not Guilty." Had it been a Black Panther Unit or Antifa Comrades, i wonder if the verdict would have been the same. These are the forces We see hiding behind the law or badge killing New Afrikan folk and poor folk all over the country while screaming . . . STOP RESISTING!! Do you understand?

People talk about God, but sanction unGodly Acts! People talk about forgiveness, but demand that prisoners not be treated like human beings. They oppose the release of PPs and POWs who have been in prison, often locked in high security or supermax prisons, incarcerated for thirty to fifty-plus years for fighting for the liberation and freedom of all oppressed people. These same reactionaries will critique and demand that We are denied access to education while in prison, that We not be allowed to transform Ourselves, to mentally grow and become a better human being and future asset to Our communities. Apparently, this is considered catering to inmates to allow such. These reactionaries are some of the same people who screamed and hollered about being locked down in their homes and cities during the height of Covid.

These same reactionaries turn a blind eye to the ghettos and barrios in this country that look like Third World Countries and then blame the victim for mismanagement, red lining, gentrification, unequal distribution of resources and neocolonial policies that affect these communities. Yet with a straight face and all the religious pride of a POPE, these reactionaries shed crocodile tears for the crimes against humanity and war taking place in Ukraine, willing to spend billions and send military aid for them to fight for their purported freedom and liberation.

i wonder if these same people would share the same sentiment, if New Afrikans chose to Rise Up and pick up arms against Our oppression. If there was just one too many George Floyds, Breonna Taylors, or one too many Michigan cops pressing a gun to the back of my head, as i am face down, and shooting me in the head? Would you feel so emotional and forthcoming if We finally got tired of the racist attacks and seeing Our sons and daughters marched into the PIC with life sentences as little "Johnny" from a "Good Family" got a slap on the wrist?

What if the resistance was coming from Afrikan countries or say Cuba or some other Third World Nations that the u.s. govt has destabilized and oppressed for centuries, like Haiti—whose legacy and history don't nobody f-kin talk about or even mention on mainstream corporate owned media? What if they wanted to send New Afrikans

Military Aid, some drones and tank busters to support Us to roll back Putin, Trump, Mitch McConnell, or Lindsay Graham? If We wanted to Free The Land!! Would you be so supportive? Would you share the resources and shed the same tears or have the same moral outrage?

What if We wanted to bring the fight to the neo-Nazis, the Proud Boys, and "good ol' boy" "Patriots" that attacked the u.s. capitol before they get too strong, consolidate, and finally move against communities of color and trigger the so-called race-war that they all say they want? Hmmm. . . .

Would the word "Genocide" so easily roll off the lips of the Oppressident Biden when it applies to New Afrikan folk like it did for Ukraine? A question all the more relevant since under trump the u.s. government withdrew from the United Nations International Treaty and Covenant Against Genocide.

Dare to Struggle—Dare to Win!!!

THE NEW AFRIKAN CREED

The New Afrikan Creed was initially adopted in 1969 and last amended in 1993. The version below includes an edited proposed, but not voted on, by the Rebuild Collective.[46]

The New Afrikan Creed

1) i believe in the spirituality, humanity, and genius of Black People, and in Our new pursuit of these values.
2) i believe in the family and the community, and in the community as a family, and i will work to make this concept live.
3) i believe in the community as more important than the individual.
4) i believe in constant struggle for freedom, to end oppression and build a better world. i believe in collective struggle; in fashioning victory in concert with my brothers and sisters.
5) i believe that the fundamental reason Our oppression continues is that We, as a people, lack the power to control Our lives.
6) i believe that the fundamental way to gain that power, and end oppression, is to build a sovereign Black Nation.
7) i believe that all the land in amerika, upon which We have lived for a long time, which We have worked and

built upon, and which We have fought to stay on, is land that belongs to Us as a people.

8) i believe in the Malcolm X Doctrine: that We must organize upon this land, and hold a plebiscite, to tell the world by a vote that We are free and Our land independent, and that after the vote, We must stand ready to defend Ourselves, establishing the nation beyond contradiction.

9) Therefore, i pledge to struggle without cease until We have won sovereignty. i pledge to struggle without fail until We have built a better condition than the world has yet known.

10) i will give my life, if that is necessary. i will give my time, my mind, my strength, and my wealth because this is necessary.

11) i will follow my chosen leaders and help them.

12) i will love my brothers and sisters as myself.

13) i will steal nothing from a brother or sister, cheat no brother or sister, misuse no brother or sister, inform on no brother or sister, and spread no gossip.

14) i will keep myself clean in body, dress, and speech, knowing that i am a light set on a hill, a true representative of what We are building.

15) i will be patient and uplifting with my brothers & sisters, and i will seek by word and by deed to heal the black family; to bring into the movement and into the community, mothers and fathers, brothers and sisters left by the wayside.

Now, freely and of my own will, i pledge this creed, for the sake of freedom for my people and a better world, on pain of disgrace and banishment if i prove false. For i am—by the inspiration of Our ancestors and the Grace of Our Creator—a New Afrikan.

THE NEW AFRIKAN DECLARATION OF INDEPENDENCE

WE, [New Afrikan] people in amerika, in consequence of arriving at a knowledge of Ourselves as a people with dignity, long deprived of that knowledge; as a consequence of revolting with every decimal of Our collective and individual beings against the oppression that for three hundred years has destroyed and broken and warped the bodies and minds and spirits of Our people in amerika, in consequence of Our raging desire to be free of this oppression, to destroy this oppression wherever it assaults mankind in the world, and in consequence of Our indistinguishable determination to go a different way, to build a new and better world, do hereby declare Ourselves forever free and independent of the jurisdiction of the united states of amerika and the obligations which that country's unilateral decision to make Our ancestors and Ourselves paper-citizens placed on Us.

We claim no rights from the united states of amerika other than those rights belonging to human beings anywhere in the world, and these include the right to damages, reparations due Us for the grievous injuries sustained by Our ancestors and Ourselves by reason of the united states' lawlessness.

Ours is a revolution against Our oppression and that of all people in the world. And it is a revolution for a better life, a better station for mankind, a surer harmony with the forces of life in the universe. We therefore, see these as the aims of Our revolution:

- To free [New Afrikan] People in amerika from oppression;

- To support and wage the world revolution until all people everywhere are so free;
- To build a new Society that is better than what We now know and as perfect as man can make it;
- To assure all people in the New Society maximum opportunity and equal access to that maximum;
- To promote industriousness, responsibility, scholarship, and service;
- To create conditions in which freedom of religion abounds and man's pursuit of god and/or the destiny, place, and purpose of man in the Universe will be without hindrance;
- To build a [New Afrikan] independent nation where no sect or religious creed subverts or impedes the building of the New Society, the New State Government, or the achievement of the Aims of the Revolution as set forth in this Declaration;
- To end exploitation of man by man or his environment;
- To assure equality of rights for the sexes;
- To end color and class discrimination, while not abolishing salubrious diversity, and to promote self-respect and mutual respect among all people in the Society;
- To protect and promote the personal dignity and integrity of the individual, and his natural rights;
- To assure justice for all;
- To place the major means of production and trade in the trust of the state to assure the benefits of this earth and man's genius and labor to society and all its members; and
- To encourage and reward the individual for hard work and initiative and insight and devotion to the Revolution.

In mutual trust and great expectation, We the undersigned, for Ourselves and for those who look to Us but who are unable personally to fix their signatures hereto, do join in this solemn Declaration of Independence, and to support this Declaration and to assure the success of Our Revolution, We pledge, without reservation, Ourselves, Our talents, and all Our worldly goods.

POLITICAL GLOSSARY

absolute egalitarianism
The narrow and fixed view that "all things are equal" and that every situation, person, or policy should be approached and dealt with in a uniform manner regardless of actual circumstances, conditions, and needs.

agent provocateur
One who joins a group in order to encourage its members to commit illegal acts for which they are then busted. They pretend to be sympathetic toward the aims of the group that they infiltrate.

amerikan ideology
Economic development regardless of the cost to human beings; a few advancing at the expense of everyone else, and all whites advancing on the backs of Black people and other peoples of color.

anarchism
The philosophy of total freedom without any governmental structure or state, rejecting the necessity of a dictatorship of the proletariat to reeducate and organize the masses and protect the gains of the revolution as a transitory stage in the development towards communism, when the state will have withered away.

automation
The process of using mechanical or electronic machines to do routine repetitive work automatically instead of employing human hands and minds.

Black
A political designation to refer not only to Afro-Americans but to people of color who are engaged in revolutionary work in the u.s. and globally. It should not be taken to mean the domination of Afro-Americans upon other people of color or the exclusion of them from Black revolutionary organizations.

Black collaborator
Those few Black people brought into the capitalist system at various levels, including such high levels as Black capitalists, project directors, administrators, etc., who have enough of a stake in the operation of the system to cooperate in pacification programs against their Black kin.

Black Revolutionary Power
The taking of state power by Black amerikans in order to revolution-ize the entire country on the basis of their enriched concept of being.

bourgeoisie
The rich and super rich. They are the ruling elite who own and manage the means of production, and the real rulers in a capitalist society. They dictate policy and have the common people working for them or enslaved by them under threat of violence, starvation, or death. The proletariat, or working class, must sell their labor power to the bourgeoisie in order to survive and then turn around and give it all right back in the form of cost of living, rent, food, etc.

cadre
A nucleus of trained, experienced activists in an organization capable of assuming leadership and/or training and education, guiding others to perform functional roles in the revolution.

civil rights
Domestic rights extended to the colonized or oppressed by the oppressor state, which can be taken away or repealed at any time. Civil rights keep the oppressed playing within the arena of those who have the power.

cliqueism
The tendency to form into little groups based upon subjective and often opportunistic alliances, which negates overall organizational unity.

collective
A cooperative unit or organization that utilizes its strength in unity to struggle for common goals and objectives.

colonialism
Foreign domination of a country or people where the economic, political, and military structure is controlled and run by the occupying force (see also "domestic colonialism").

communism
A social system based on collective ownership of the means of production and the absence of classes or a state apparatus.

constructive criticism
The positive identification and correction of mistaken ideas and incorrect practices by offering practical solutions that builds others up rather than tearing them down.

contradiction
The basic two-sidedness of all things which consists of a clash between opposites; the internal struggle in all phenomena that spurs growth, development, and transformation.

coup d'état
The successful overthrow of existing authority in one audacious stroke, usually by a section of the armed forces or another small well-organized grouping. This can result in political power falling into the lap of a rival, pro-imperialist group.

counterrevolutionary
Someone or something that goes against revolutionary principles and practices.

democratic centralism
The unity between freedom and discipline. Within any revolutionary organization requires both democracy and centralism. Under democratic centralism, group members are afforded the freedom to speak their opinion, make suggestions, and criticize any errors on all levels in order to strengthen the unity and discipline of the whole. The whole is duty-bound to carry out decisions made despite their individual stance to maintain unity.

dialectics
The scientific, analytical approach to studying the contradictions within every phenomenon. Dialectics takes into account the historical development and interaction of interrelated things, holding that nothing exists independent, isolated, or unconnected from others; that all are connected and part of a whole system and are dependent on and determined by others. Accordingly, dialectics understands that all things are in a constant state of motion and change. Changes on a small enough level begin with a quantitative character before, after a certain point, the degree of change becomes qualitative and the overall essence or character of the thing is different.

domestic colonialism
A new and higher or more advanced stage of colonialism. When direct oppressive rule (e.g. segregation/apartheid) becomes threatened, colonialism must move to the next stage and incorporate some of the natives and the oppressed into the system in order to further legitimize its oppressive rule and preserve the status quo, thereby attempting to stave off and/or misdirect any serious threat to its continued rule. The use of "Black faces in high places" as a cover for white power is an example of domestic, or neocolonialism. The u.s. is a prison house of many nations denied the right to Self-Determination. Domestic colonialism is when the u.s. government oppresses its internal colonies, such as the New Afrikan/Black Nation for continued super-economic and social exploitation. This includes seizing and

controlling its means of production and forcing Us to sell Our labor power for the benefit of the oppressive state.

dogmatic
A person, group, or belief system that is rigid and unbending, neglecting to consider changing conditions or the differences between situations and circumstances.

empire
In these modern times, it represents the highest stage of development of a capitalist nation. It is characterized by expanding spheres of influence throughout the world using military coups and financial-economic means to gain control over peoples and lands.

fascism
A repressive form of government that takes on police-state characteristics, in that all forms of political, economic, and social opposition are forcibly suppressed to maintain the status quo.

forces of production
In order to produce, instruments of production are necessary like tools, machines, means of transport, etc. But these do not produce anything by themselves. The forces of production, therefore, consist of the instruments of production as well as people, with their production experience and skill, who use these instruments.

freedom
The right to understand the world, the environment, and the forces acting on Us with agency to deal with these circumstances so that We may harmonize as a people and develop to a higher level.

historical materialism
The dialectical and materialist approach to understanding the history and development of society by examining the source and origins of social ideas, theories, political philosophies, and institutions—the spiritual life of society—which is determined by the conditions of the material life of society.

idealism
The concept that states the mind is primary and matter is secondary; that all things originate from the idea and that matter is only a reflection of what exists in the mind, as one perceives it. In idealism, the physical world can only be conceived as relative to or dependent on mental image.

ideology
A system set on principles and beliefs relating to life, culture, politics, etc. Integrated assertions, theories, and aims that constitute a socio-political program.

ideological struggle
The conflict, fought through rhetoric and practice rather than physical aggression, between different ideologies in trying to prove themselves correct and those opposing incorrect.

imperialism
The exploitation, rape, and subsequent oppression practiced by one nation over another for greed and profit. The extension of capitalism into the international arena.

individualism
A narrow, selfish approach or outlook based upon putting oneself before the interest of the people, organization, and comrades. A bourgeois tendency expressed in the "bootstrap" theory.

irresponsible criticism
Frivolous and irrelevant correcting or pointing out of minor and needless points, which instead of building tears down and obstructs progressive growth and development; nitpicking which tends to sidetrack one from what really has to be done; ungrounded and unfounded criticism; criticizing without investigation and thinking first.

lackey
A flunky or footman. Also: to wait upon or serve slavishly.

liberation
The state of freedom from a repressive or exploitative existence, where the people have gained control of their own lives and the right to self-determination.

lumpenproletariat
The underclass, unemployed, marginally employed and those who live outside of the law such as the "criminal" element. The aged, infirm, and disabled are also part of this class because they are marginally employed and therefore not a secure part of the productive process. Those on welfare and social security are also members of this class.

means of production
The means by which capitalism, for example, undertakes production: normally including factories, industrial plants in which to produce, machinery and tools with which to fashion raw materials, and the new materials themselves, including auxiliary materials such as fuel and oil.

mode of production
The way in which people produce and exchange their means of life. Every society is based on this, which ultimately determines the character of all social activities and institutions. The mode of production is always social, for the material goods required by the community are produced by the labor of many, who carry on a mutual exchange of activities in producing the social product which is distributed among the community. The forces of production enter into certain relations of production in order for the forces of production to be applied according to the different relations of production. Examples: slavery, feudalism, capitalism, socialism, communism.

neocolonialism
Foreign domination of a country or people by an imperialist power where the economic, political, and military structure is run by a native bourgeoisie. The imperialists maintain control of the economy because they continue to own the means of production, and the client state is totally dependent, military and politically, on the imperialists for their survival.

New Afrikan
The revolutionary national identity of the Afro-American or Black person born within the u.s.a., or a citizen of the People's Republic of New Afrika (the Black Belt Region).

oppression
Unjust and cruel exercise of authority to deny people their human rights and their right to a decent, healthy life. Intolerable living conditions such as inadequate health, education, medical care, housing, etc.

petit-bourgeoisie
The middle-class or privileged worker who enjoys a relatively comfortable level of existence: the small businessmen, entrepreneurs, and self-employed. Artists, entertainers, doctors, lawyers, and athletes being in this class. They do not own or control the major means of production but their main aspiration is to obtain the status, wealth, and power of the bourgeoisie.

politics
A process by which the political and social decisions involving the organization of society are made and the method of solving political contradictions.

principles
The fundamental grounds on which a human being, organization, movement, cause, or concept stands. Its basic aspects are expressed in terms of rules, codes, ethics, laws, and statements of philosophical truths which explain all examined natural, social, and universal spheres and guide human thought and action to transforming the human world for the benefit of the human being.

proletariat
The largest class which comprises the majority of the working masses, who must sell their labor power in order to survive. They represent the lowest level of the employed with the lowest wages, benefits, and rights, who usually have little or no power or control of their working conditions, management or planning. It is the class that has the most to lose due to the advent of increased technology and automation

because they are being driven out of their jobs into the ranks of the unemployed. Marx classified them as the most potentially revolutionary class because of their sheer numbers as well as their social consciousness and needs which are directly tied to the whole process of production.

propaganda
The publicized activity by which the party or revolutionary organization politicizes the masses. Can also be enemy misinformation or disinformation with the intent to misdirect, misinform, disrupt, and distract revolutionary forces in an attempt to cause dissension within the ranks.

racism
The philosophy and practice which pursues or condones the systematic oppression of another race because that oppressed race is believed inferior.

reactionary
Characterized by a tendency toward rolling back and repressing changes to the status quo. Includes those forces which oppose revolutionary change and actively work to prevent or destroy any progressive movement, country, etc.

reformism
The amending and making of internal changes within a system, such as by changing laws or introducing and funding poverty programs for the people without changing the whole system for what it is.

relations of production
These are relations in which people of a given society must arrange and enter into by necessity to perpetuate human existence. Since the birth of class societies, these relations have long existed where the property holders came to exercise a relationship of dominance, exploitation, and wealth over the propertyless. Other forms of these relations are between master and slave, feudal lord and serf, landlord and peasant, capitalist and worker, etc.

revisionism
Deviation from and manipulation or modification of the correct revolutionary line (or of any particular belief or practice) to suit one's own personal vested interest. Revisionism often results from or contributes to cliqueism.

socialism
A social system where the means of production are owned collectively by the people through a state, where the basis for production is for the people's welfare, not profit. The people are organized on all levels of society and play an active role in the management and decision-making process. The people's right to the basic necessities of life is protected and most social services such as education, health and child care are free. The people are represented by a people's government dedicated to upholding the principles of socialism and serving the people and humanity unselfishly, courageous of sacrifice, and free from corruption. People work and contribute to society according to their needs and abilities. There is no oppressed class and the rulers are the people themselves; no huge corporations or private ownership of the means of production, industry, social services, etc. A society where the profit motive has been replaced with the concern for mankind.

united front
A long-term alliance of social classes and groups like women, queer people, youth, and elders, or different factions of a cultural, regional, or political space to focus on a clear-cut political program.

unity
The working together of two separate entities.

Unity-Criticism-Unity
The process of the members of a group, unit, or organization uniting on a set of principles and objectives to struggle internally and privately among themselves by working together, observing and analyzing each other's errors and then offering constructive criticism to each other to correct errors and overcome any shortcomings in order to strengthen each other and thus advance the group towards its stated objectives. This is a continuous process of transforming old unities to

new ones in a neverending process. Any organized body must engage in principled unity, criticism, and practice if it wishes to succeed in accomplishing its stated objectives.

ACKNOWLEDGMENTS

This book wouldn't have been possible without the vital assistance of so many organizations, coalitions, groups, publications, networks, and individuals who have helped me not only survive inside these tombs but continue organizing, educating, learning, and developing throughout the decades of captivity. These are the same people and collectives who have, are, and will continue fighting for the abolition of the PIC and the imperialist, neocolonialist, capitalist structures it serves.

Listing every individual and grouping would be a book unto itself, so forgive me for any that are omitted.

But i would first like to acknowledge all the comrades in the New Afrikan Independence Movement, fallen and alive, and outlets and organizations like the Spear and Shield/Re-Build Collective, *San Francisco Bay View*, the August Third Collective—NAPLA NAIM, New Afrikan Liberation Collective, the Spirit of Mandela, Prison Lives Matter, and Free Kwame "Beans" Shakur.

i've been sustained and energized by working with my comrades in IDOC Watch, the Indianapolis Liberation Center, Northwest Indiana Coalition to Abolish Control Unit Prisons; the Jericho Movement; Prison Lives Matter; the Forty Strong; Hear Her Voice; FOCUS Initiatives, LTD.; *In the Belly*; the *Virginia Defender*; Party for Socialism and Liberation; Prison Riot Radio; *Prison Legal News*; *Hood Communist*; the Black Alliance for Peace; *Black Agenda Report*; Anarchist Black Cross (especially the James River grouping as of late); Millennials are Killing Capitalism; the Committee to End the Marion Lockdown; the Incarcerated Workers Organizing Committee; Malcolm

X Grassroots Movement; Jailhouse Lawyers Speak; Hampton Insti-
tute; Abolition Law Center; the Free Alabama Movement; Critical
Resistance; Hands off Haiti Solidarity Committee; ANSWER Coa-
lition (Act Now to Stop War and End Racism); Kite Line Radio;
Beyond Prisons Podcast; Iskra Books; Black Power Media; *Where the
River Flows*; Indy Hope Packages; Georgia College & State University
Mutual Aid Society; Democratic Socialists of DePauw; Black Lives
Matter North West Indiana; and so many others.

No movement that leaves its PPs and POWs behind is worth its
salt, and there are many—but not enough—people who sustain this
work through or outside of various organizations, including Seth
Donnelly, Maurice Robinson, Wednesday Jin, my comrades who
made it out alive like Leon Benson, and my comrades outside these
bars but still not free, like Vernon T. Bateman.

HOW TO SUPPORT THE SHAKA SHAKUR FREEDOM CAMPAIGN

As the reader now knows, Shaka A. Shakur is a significant New Afrikan Political Prisoner, revolutionary organizer, leader, theorist, and movement builder. He is a longtime fighter for the liberation of the Republic of New Afrika and all oppressed peoples. Shaka has been held captive by the state of Indiana since 2002, when they imprisoned him on trumped-up charges for which Shaka has already served his initial sentence. The real reason he remains a Political Prisoner is because of his central role as an organizer within, across, and beyond prison bars.

What You Can Do Now

Go to ShakaShakur.org to:
- Sign a Petition for Shaka's Clemency
- Get Involved in the Campaign
- Join an Existing Chapter or Start One
- Donate to the Legal Fund
- Write to Shaka (you can email him at Shaka@ShakaShakur.org)

About the Shaka Shakur Freedom Campaign

While Shaka's support network and organizing date back decades, the Shaka Shakur Freedom Campaign emerged as an official 501(c)(3) in 2024. Its origins lie in the creation of Free Shaka Shakur, which was formed when a key organization Shaka co-founded, FOCUS Initiatives, first joined the Indianapolis Liberation Center in December 2023.[47]

The Indianapolis Liberation Center is a physical and virtual community hub advancing the struggles of all oppressed, exploited, and dispossessed people in Indianapolis and beyond by uniting and working to overcome the divisions imposed on Us by the oppressing classes. Through collaboration and regular political, cultural, educational, and other programming, it facilitates the training of new revolutionary fighters, helps all involved develop to higher levels, and fosters a collectivity that realizes the necessity and possibility of revolutionary transformation.[48]

When Free Shaka Shakur joined the Center, it was a crucial step toward overcoming one of the most difficult obstacles in uniting Our people: the division between those outside and behind enemy lines. As a result of the Center's dynamism—to which Free Shaka Shakur did not add but multiply—within a year it grew into the nationwide Shaka Shakur Freedom Campaign, which has chapters across the prison house of nations called the u.s. The Campaign's national headquarters is located at the Indianapolis Liberation Center.

ENDNOTES

Editorial Introduction

1   See Ned Oliver, "As Prisoners Continue to Die, Virginia Appeals Federal Court Order Mandating Better Health Care," *Virginia Mercury*, August 19, 2019. https://virginiamercury.com/2019/08/14/as-prisoners-continue-to-die-virginia-appeals-court-order-mandating-better-healthcare; and Dale Brumfield, "Why Did Kiki Webb Have to Die?" *Virginia Mercury*, September 7, 2023. https://virginiamercury.com/2023/09/07/why-did-kiki-webb-have-to-die.

2   There were a total of ten inmates rounded up, although four had charges dropped. See "Who Are the Indiana Six?" www.shakashakur.org/who-are-the-indiana-6.

3   Shaka A. Shakur, "No Right to Speak!," in ibid., 3.

4   Sanyika Shakur, *Stand Up Struggle Forward: New Afrikan Revolutionary Writings on Nation, Class and Patriarch*y (Montreal: Kersplebedeb, 2013), 91.

Preface

5   Sanyika Shakur, "An Open Response Letter to the New Afrikan Black Panther Party with Regard to its Position Paper Titled: 'Black Liberation in the 21st Century: A Revolutionary Reassessment of Black Nationalism,'" *Kersplebedeb*, February 16, 2013. Available here: kersplebedeb.com/posts/aa3-to-nabpp-critique.

6   The last words George Jackson spoke before his assassination were reportedly, "The dragon has come," a reference to a short poem by Ho Chi Minh, which ends with, "When. The prison doors are opened, the real. Dragon will fly out." See Ho Chi Minh, "Word Play," in *Ho Chi Minh on Revolution: Selected Writings, 1920–66*, ed. Bernard B. Fall (New York: Signet Books, 1968), 137.

Introduction

7   George Jackson, *Soledad Brothers: The Prison Letters of George Jackson* (Chicago: Lawrence Hill Books, 1970/1994), 127.

Section I: The Personal Is Political
1. Many Are Called But Few Are Chosen

8   Although the bulk of this article appeared around 2016, we have updated Shaka's age and number of years in captivity to reflect the manuscript submission of January 2025.

5. Moving Towards Atonement: Men, Masculinity and Love

9   bell hooks, *The Will to Change: Men, Masculinity, and Love* (New York: Atria Books, 2004), 18.

10   Cited in Ibid., 23.

Section II: History, Theory, and Practice
6. The New Afrikan Independence Movement and the Republic of New Afrika

11   Jalil A. Muntaqim, *We Are Our Own Liberators: Selected Prison Writings* (Portland: Arissa Media Group, 2010).

12   Marcus Garvey, *Philosophy and Opinions of Marcus Garvey*, ed. A. Jacques-Garvey (New York: Atheneum, 1986), 126.

13   Muntaqim, *We Are Our Own Liberators*, 109–156.

14   United Nations, *Universal Declaration of Human Rights* (New York: United Nations, 2015), 32.

15   The New Afrikan Liberation Collective (NALC) was founded around 2015 in the Pendleton "Correctional" Facility, one of the most infamous of Indiana's numerous repressive institutions. Its founders, Kwame "Beans" Shakur and Shaka Shakur, established the collective—one of several groupings—to continue the development and flourishing of the struggle for the Liberation of New Afrikans and the creation of the Republic of New Afrika.

16   A Swahili motto, Vita Wa Watu is generally translated into English as "People's War." In 1986, after the seventh and last edition of the journal, "Notes from a New Afrikan POW," the *Vita Wa Watu* journal inherited the legacy as the theoretical Afrikan Independence Movement.

17   The following citations of international law come from the following sources: UN General Assembly, "Convention on the Prevention and Punishment of the Crime of Genocide," 260 (III) (Paris, 1948); UN General Assembly, "Programme of Action for the Full Implementation of the Declaration on the Granting of Independence to Colonial Countries and Peoples," 2621 XXV (New York, 1970); and UN General Assembly, "International Covenant on Economic, Social and Cultural Rights," 2200 XXI (New York, 1966).

18   The u.s. did not ratify the Genocide convention until November 5, 1988, forty years after the founding document was enshrined into international law. Further, the u.s. signed it with the reservation that its officials, representatives, and ostensibly citizens would be immune from prosecution under it unless the u.s. government consented.

7. An Honest Conversation and Self-Critique

19 This chapter was initially published as part of an opening series of essays establishing the New Afrikan Liberation Collective (NALC) as an independent ideological tendency within the NAIM.

8. Tactics and Strategies in the Struggle for Independence

20 Like the last chapter, this is one of the foundational texts Shaka wrote for the New Afrikan Liberation Collective.

10. Prison Abolitionism: Tailoring the Message

21 Amos N. Wilson, *Black-On-Black Violence: The Psychodynamics of Black Self-Annihilation in Service of White Domination* (New York: Afrikan World Infosystems, 1994), 57–58.

22 UN General Assembly, "United Nations Standard Minimum Rules for the Treatment of Prisoners (the Nelson Mandela Rules)," A/RES/70/175, January 8, 2016.

23 Cited Wilson, *Black-on-Black Violence*, 13.

Section III: The Prison Industrial Complex
11. The Struggle against Organized White Supremacy in Indiana Prisons

24 Shaka A. Shakur first published this piece in February 2020. For more context on the subject, see Kelsey Kauffman, *The Brotherhood: Racism and Intimidation Among Prison Staff at the Indiana Correctional Facility – Putnamville* (Greencastle, IN: Russel J. Compton Center for Peace and Justice, 2001). Also available at: www.shakashakur.org/the-brotherhood.

25 See IDOC Watch, "Shaka Shakur Charged with Attacking Guard at Wabash Valley, Indiana: Calls Needed Now!" *IDOC Watch*, September 19, 2017. Available at: www.idocwatch.org/shakur-charged.

26 Where the River Flows, "Shaka Shakur On Hunger Strike Victory in Indiana Prison," *It's Going Down*, January 2, 2018, available here: itsgoingdown.org/shaka-shakur-hunger-strike-victory-indiana-prison.

27 Balagoon and Naeem, known as "The Pendleton Two," are currently serving 82- and 142-year sentences for saving the life of Lincoln Love, a fellow inmate prison guards affiliated with the Sons of Light (a KKK-splinter group) were trying to murder. For more information visit the Pendleton Two Defense Committee's website, www.pendleton2.com.

28 Putnamville was called the Indiana State Farm and is now named the Putnamville Correctional Facility.

29 *Prison News Service* also played an instrumental role in that mass work and politicization – Shaka A. Shakur.

12. Reawakening a Sleeping Giant

30 IDOC Watch, "Kwame Shakur brutally assaulted by guards at Pendleton Correctional Facility, Indiana," *San Francisco Bay View*, January 31, 2018, available here: indyliberationcenter.org/kwame-attack-2018.

31   The *Prison Lives Matter* journal turned out to be one of many publications and projects organized by the organization, which continues to play a key role in the prison struggle. See supportprisonlives.org.

14. Domestic Exile: Low-Intensity Warfare

32   This essay was first released on January 4, 2021.

33   Cited in Joshua Bloom and Walden E. Martin Jr., *Black Against Empire: The History and Politics of the Black Panther Party* (Berkeley: University of California Press, 2013), 210-211.

34   Ruchell Magee was one of the longest-held Political Prisoners in the world when he was finally released in 2023, the same year he passed away.

35   During its fifteen years of activity, between 1985–2000, the Committee to End the Marion Lockdown produced newsletters including *Walkin' Steel* and, in collaboration with the National Campaign to Stop Control Unit Prisons *ABOLISH!* You can read more about the group in Nancy Kurshan's, *Out of Control: A 15-Year Battle Against Control Unit Prisons* (Berkeley: Freedom Archives, 2013).

36   This refers to the Human Rights Campaign's publication, *Cold Storage: Super-Maximum Security Confinement in Indiana* (New York: Human Rights Watch, 1997).

37   Needless to say, with the rise of formations such as the New Afrikan Black Panther – Prison Chapter, New Afrikan Liberation Collective, various formations in Cali that were born out of the massive prison hunger strikes and Pelican Bay resistance and general strikes nationally—the state strategy has failed! –Shaka A. Shakur

38   Michelle Alexander, *The New Jim Crow: Mass Incarceration in the Age of Colorblindness* (New York: The New Press, 2010). For critiques of Alexander's book, see Greg Thomas, "Why Some Like *The New Jim Crow* So Much," *imixwhatilike*, April 26, 2012, available here: imixwhatilike.org/2012/04/26/whysomelikethenewjimcrowsomuch; and Eugene Puryear, *Shackled and Chained: Mass Incarceration in Capitalist America* (San Francisco: PSL Publications, 2013).

39   As of this writing (December 2024), Kevin "Rashid" Johnson is currently held at Red Onion Supermax Prison in Virginia where, like all supermax prisons, conditions are so bad that numerous prisoners have set themselves on fire in an attempt to get transferred.

40   See, for a recent example, Leon Benson, *Letters of Gratitude: i AM Because We Are* (Madison: Iskra Books: 2024).

41   See Muntaqim, *We Are Own Liberators*. FROLINAN stands for the Front for the Liberation of the New Afrikan Nation.

Section IV: Continuing the Struggle
15. The Struggle for Education Behind the Walls

42   Shaka wrote this piece in September 2024, shortly after he was shipped from Beaumont Correctional Center to another Virginia prison, Buckingham Correctional Center.

16. Palestine and the New Afrikan (Black) Nation

43   At the request of Indianapolis organizers, Shaka wrote this text for the February 17, 2024, Global Day of Action for Palestine. In Indianapolis and over one hundred other

cities throughout six continents, the ANSWER Coalition (Act Now to Stop War and End Racism), Jewish Voice for Peace, Party for Socialism and Liberation, Palestinian Youth Movement, and others organized the coordinated protests. Lead organizers played Shaka's recorded statement outside of the Lucas Oil Field Stadium, which was hosting NBA All-Star Weekend. As the audience heard Shaka's statement, their cheers grew louder than the speakers playing his message. See Liberator Staff, "During NBA All-Star Weekend, Indy Keeps all Eyes on Rafah!," *Indianapolis Liberation Center*, February 18, 2024, available here: indyliberationcenter.org/nba-rafah; and David Zirin, "To Find Excitement at the NBA All-Star Game, Look to the Stands," *The Nation*, February 20, 2024, available at: thenation.com/article/society/nba-all-star-game-gaza-ceasefire.

17. Revolutionary Notes from the Western Front

44 This essay was published on May 17, 2024 on the website of the Shaka Shakur Freedom Campaign.

18. Signposts on the Road to Freedom

45 Wilson, *Black-On-Black Violence*, xiii, xvii.

Appendix A: The New Afrikan Creed

46 "Deaf, dumb, and blind" have been replaced by "my brothers and sisters" in point fifteen and removed from the last paragraph. This reflects proposed amendments to the Creed made by members of the Rebuild Collective. These proposed amendments have also been forwarded to, but not voted on, by the People's Center Council of the Provisional Government of the Republic of New Afrika.

How to Support the Shaka Shakur Freedom Campaign

47 More information at: ShakaShakur.org/ShakaILC.

48 More information at: IndyLiberationCenter.org.

BIBLIOGRAPHY

Alexander, Michelle. *The New Jim Crow: Mass Incarceration in the Age of Colorblindness.* New York: The New Press, 2010.

Benson, Leon. *Letters of Gratitude: i AM Because We Are.* Madison: Iskra Books: 2024.

Bloom, Joshua and Walden E. Martin Jr. *Black Against Empire: The History and Politics of the Black Panther Party.* Berkeley: University of California Press, 2013.

Brumfield, Dale. "Why Did Kiki Webb Have to Die?" *Virginia Mercury,* September 7, 2023. Available at: virginiamercury.com/2023/09/07/why-did-kiki-webb-have-to-die.

Garvey, Marcus. *Philosophy and Opinions of Marcus Garvey.* Edited by A. Jacques-Garvey. New York: Atheneum, 1986.

Ho Chi Minh, *Ho Chi Minh on Revolution: Selected Writings, 1920–66,* ed. Bernard B. Fall. New York: Signet Books, 1968.

hooks, bell. *The Will to Change: Men, Masculinity, and Love.* New York: Atria Books, 2004.

Human Rights Campaign. *Cold Storage: Super-Maximum Security Confinement in Indiana.* New York: Human Rights Watch, 1997.

IDOC Watch. "Kwame Shakur brutally assaulted by guards at Pendleton Correctional Facility, Indiana." *San Francisco Bay View,* January, 31, 2018. Available here: indyliberationcenter.org/kwame-attack-2018.

IDOC Watch. "Shaka Shakur Charged with Attacking Guard at Wabash Valley, Indiana: Calls Needed Now!" *IDOC Watch,* September 19, 2017. Available at: www.idocwatch. org/shakur-charged.

Jackson, George. *Soledad Brothers: The Prison Letters of George Jackson.* Chicago: Lawrence Hill Books, 1970/1994.

Kauffman, Kelsey. *The Brotherhood: Racism and Intimidation Among Prison Staff at the Indiana Correctional Facility – Putnamville.* Greencastle: Russel J. Compton Center for Peace and Justice, 2001.

Kurshan Nancy. *Out of Control: A 15-Year Battle Against Control Unit Prisons.* Berkeley: Freedom Archives, 2013.

Liberator Staff. "During NBA All-Star Weekend, Indy Keeps all Eyes on Rafah!,"
    Indianapolis Liberation Center, February 18, 2024. Available here: indyliberationcenter.
    org/nba-rafah.

Muntaqim, Jalil A. *We Are Our Own Liberators: Selected Prison Writings*. Portland: Arissa
    Media Group, 2000.

Oliver, Ned. "As Prisoners Continue to Die, Virginia Appeals Federal
    Court Order Mandating Better Health Care," *Virginia Mercury*,
    August 19, 2019. Available at: virginiamercury.com/2019/08/14/
    as-prisoners-continue-to-die-virginia-appeals-court-order-mandating-better-healthcare.

Puryear, Eugene. *Shackled and Chained: Mass Incarceration in Capitalist America*. San
    Francisco: Liberation Media, 2013.

Shakur, Sanyika. "An Open Response Letter to the New Afrikan Black Panther Party
    with Regard to its Position Paper Titled: 'Black Liberation in the 21st Century: A
    Revolutionary Reassessment of Black Nationalism,'" *Kersplebedeb*, February 16, 2013.
    Available here: kersplebedeb.com/posts/aa3-to-nabpp-critique.

Shakur, Sanyika. *Stand Up Struggle Forward: New Afrikan Revolutionary Writings on
    Nation, Class and Patriarchy*. Montreal: Kersplebedeb, 2013.

Thomas, Greg. "Why Some Like *The New Jim Crow* So Much." *imixwhatilike*,
    April 26, 2012. Available here: imixwhatilike.org/2012/04/26/
    whysomelikethenewjimcrowsomuch.

United Nations. *Universal Declaration of Human Rights*. New York: United Nations, 2015.

United Nations General Assembly. "Convention on the Prevention and Punishment of the
    Crime of Genocide." 260 (III). Paris, 1948.

United Nations General Assembly. "International Covenant on Economic, Social, and
    Cultural Rights." 2200 (XXI). New York, 1966.

United Nations General Assembly. "Programme of Action for the Full Implementation of
    the Declaration on the Granting of Independence to Colonial Countries and Peoples."
    2621 (XXV). New York, 1970.

Where the River Flows. "Shaka Shakur On Hunger Strike Victory in Indiana Prison."
    It's Going Down, January 2, 2018. Available at: https://itsgoingdown.org/
    shaka-shakur-hunger-strike-victory-indiana-prison.

Wilson, Amos N. *Black-On-Black Violence: The Psychodynamics of Black Self-Annihilation
    in Service of White Domination,* 4th printing. New York: Afrikan World Infosystems,
    1994. New York: Afrikan World Infosystems.

Zirin, David. "To Find Excitement at the NBA All-Star Game, Look to the Stands."
    The Nation, February 20, 2024. Available at: thenation.com/article/society/
    nba-all-star-game-gaza-ceasefire.